EmbalmedTime

Photography in the Post Photographic Era

FSC
www.fsc.org
MIX
Papper från ansvarsfulla källor
Paper from responsible sources
FSC® C105338

Cover photo: Uffe Berggren

English version by Uffe Berggren of the Swedish edition ”Balsamerad tid : Fotografiet i den postfotografiska eran”, BOD 2018.

Publisher: BoD – Books on Demand, Stockholm, Sverige

Printing: BoD – Books on Demand, Norderstedt, Tyskland

ISBN: 9789179698836

Embalmed Time

Photography in the Post Photographic Era

Uffe Berggren

Contents

The Starting Blocks 5

The Post Photographic Era 12

Photography: Documentation or Art Form? 41

The Peculiarities of the Photographic Image 58

The Viewer's Influence on
the Emotions of Photography 86

Creating Photography ....,.......,... 108

Street Photography Continues a Tradition of
the 'Flaneurs' 130

The Possibilities of Technology 156

Revealing the Hidden Secrets of Photographic
Images 162

Literature 193

Le voyage d'exploration ne consiste pas à rechercher des terres nouvelles, mais à voir avec un regard neuf.

Marcel Proust: *A la recherche du temps perdu*

The Starting Blocks

Yet another book on photography? With a few decades left until it's time to celebrate photography's two-hundredth anniversary, most things should be said about photography. However, the world has changed during the last 200 years and the view of photography with it. Photography appeared on the scene during the second century of industrialism and technological advances have, during the time photography has existed, has also greatly influenced the development of photography.

However, this is not a book about the purely technical aspects of photography or image analysis as such, although this is touched upon to and fro in the texts. The focus in the following texts lies on the psychology of the seeing, the interpretation and the understanding. How photography is in its "essence" and how it affects us, are some questions I have been looking for answers to in the literature. Of course, the texts have been about how photographs are loaded with emotions and how these trigger yet another set of emotions within the viewer – emotions that can create an individual interpretation and meaning of a photograph deep down inside each and every one of us. Interesting questions, for example, are whether we really can "see" something in a photograph if we don't we have any previous experience of what we are supposed to "see".

What is a photograph, a painting or a sculpture other than a way of capturing the viewer's attention? Hopefully the author of an image has seen something in her surroundings that she wants to draw the viewer's attention to. In other words, photography can be said to be a "trap" for the eyes, and eventually for the spectator's mind. These traps can be more or less effective – the viewer must work *with* the trap for it to work. This is because we cannot see something in an "image" that we have not already seen or, we cannot detect something that we have not already imagined. If another person can "think" the content, there is the possibility that the viewer also can "see" it.

Collecting photographs is, according to Susan Sontag, collecting the world (Sontag1973:1). Whoever collects tries to establish control and by collecting images of the world we probably try to exercise control over something that it is impossible to create control over. You could say that the photographer, who "collects" by making photographs, tries to organize the world, but faces a hopeless task. Still, most photographers, professional as well as hobby photographers, are constantly making pictures that make their archives ever bigger.

How is it that photography has come to play a role in each man's life, at least in the western world? In addition to the base level, where anyone who wants an ID document has to make a photograph of themselves, there are many variations of photographs in our lives that are not necessary for our existence. Nevertheless, we are involved in the viewing of advertising images, family pictures and media images, and since the dawn of Internet there has been an explosion in the volume of images that we encounter. This is partly because we are exposed to all these photographs, without our own making, and partly because man seems to be wired to solve "riddles", where photographs can stand for many, in our surroundings. We can probably not stop ourselves, but we enter into the world of photographs and try to create context and meaning looking at them. As we enter this journey into the landscape that some writers call "magical" or "mysterious", it seems that we benefit from all the experiences we encounter in our attempts to create something similar to a personal meaning with the photograph we for the moment have the opportunity to interact with.

The photographs we make become documents that allow us to understand the world. According to sociologist Piotr Sztompka, there are two ways in which photography can be used in everyday sociology, by making photographs of social situations and by interpreting existing photographic images (Sztompka 2008:5). Making pictures has many areas of interpretation. For starters, it awakens our sensitivity to social situations, as it replaces the passive "look", where countless chaotic impressions only flow in front of our eyes, with a deliberate "look", where we consciously select and rank the images according to their significance. Three technical features of the camera are helpful here, says Sztompka. First, we must focus on something, which means choosing something of the highest importance in the observed situation. Second, we must frame the image, which means eliminating the features of the situation that are considered less important. Thirdly, we must determine the depth of field, distinguish foreground from background. This is of course everyday food for the experienced photographer, but as a collection of data for sociological research on everyday life, Piotr Sztompka tries to regard photographs as a foundation. His hope is that the study of photographs made in everyday situations will help us to describe changes and clarify existing conditions. What happens when we "make" a photographic image? A description that paints gives a painterly picture of what is happening has been made by a Mexican writer (De Haene Rosique 2009:9):

Observe, observe, capture on the mechanical retina, define exposure times, find the frame, guarantee the best angle, determine the composition, define focal length, depth of field ... fire the shutter to snatch a fragment of reality with high contrast and semitones to create an alternate reality, visible, tangible and two-dimensional. As is evident, this is no uncomplicated process. In this collection of texts, however, the focus is more on how the viewer perceives the already exposed image than how the photographer has gone about to achieve it.

As mentioned above, this is no uncomplicated process. In this collection of texts, however, the focus is more on how the viewer perceives the already exposed image than how the photographer has gone about to achieve it.

My thought is that because we, at least in the Western world, have been soaked in reproductions of photographs, photography has taken an important place in our lives, whether we like it or not. When I scouted for literature, it struck me how many different types of writers have gone about trying to interpret photography and its role in our lives. They all try to answer questions such as: where is the photograph, when is the photograph, how is the photograph and why is the photograph? One of the more intrusive questions is asked by W. J. T. Mitchell in this form: "What do pictures really want?" (Mitchell 1996). This is a question, among many, that recurs repeatedly in these texts. However, Mitchell (1994:11) has expressed concern that we do not really know what images are and how their relationship to language is, how they work for us viewers and the world, and what we should do with them. It's a bunch of demanding thoughts.

In summing up the texts in this collection, I dare to interpret the "message" in the texts. Although I did not really foresee that there would be any message in them when I started writing them some years ago. These interpretations are based on the fact that the texts are about the relationship we as viewers have with the photographic image. It is also about how the viewer loads the image with an individual content that is based on the individual's experiences and references. This is what allows us as individuals to see completely different things in a photograph.

A lot has been written about photographs and photography throughout the ages, however, the texts below do not claim to be comprehensive. However, I would like to point out that it is nothing new to think about photography and its role in our lives. Walter Benjamin, a German philosopher who wrote extensively on media in the 1930s, is an inspiration for my attempts. The thoughts in Walter Benjamin's "Little history of photography" were an expression of a deep emotional commitment to an ever-open debate about aesthetics that had been triggered by the shared hope of a social revolution, Herbert Molderings (2014:335) argues. Without the empathetic embrace of the actions of the revolutionary masses, which for a literary figure means as much as the prospects of a new audience, new tasks and purposes: Benjamin's perspective would have relinquished a great deal of their emotional impulses. As an individual expression of the historically unique and never-to-be-repeated artwork, bourgeois intelligence and Marxist labor movement appeared. Walter Benjamin's "Little History of Photography" remains a sketch that, in Herbert Moldering's opinion, cannot be completed; it is an intellectual torso where the unfinished always exists as an aesthetic form. In "Little History of Photography", Walter Benjamin undoubtedly draws a lance for photography, at least in one way. Walter Benjamin (2008:294-5) states:

"It is not the person ignorant of writing but the one ignorant of photography," somebody has said, "who will be the illiterate of the future." But mustn't the photographer who is unable to read his own pictures be no less deemed an illiterate? Isn't inscription bound to become the most essential component of the photograph? These are the questions in which the span of ninety years that separates contemporary photography from the daguerreotype discharges its historical tension. It is in the illumination of these sparks that the first photographs emerge, beautiful and unapproachable, from the darkness of our grandfathers' day.

We have seen developments with attempts to integrate image and text. Among others, Sven Lidman, who, at least for the Swedish market, coined the concept of lexivisual representation.

Photographs are only part of all the images that surround us, and there are also drawings, paintings and sculptures. I agree with Sturken & Cartwright (2001: 4-5) who wrote a textbook on visual culture:

"Visual culture should be understood, not only by historians and other 'image experts', but by all of us who increasingly encounter an astonishing collection of images in our daily lives."

The visual culture is all around us, we live immersed in it and we constantly interpret visual elements in our everyday lives.

Often the interpretation is done with a certain routine. In what follows some thoughts about the visual are presented, not just about photography. While working on these texts, I have come to develop a certain fondness for André Bazin's (1967: 14) notion that photography does not create eternity, as art does, photography embalms time, saves it from its own downfall. I have therefore called this collection texts for 'The Embalming of Time: Photography in the Postphotographic Era' – which can be said to point to one of the important features of photography – as a document that we believe shows us "what it looked like, what it was like". In addition, I became interested in the "post-photographic" about which more follows in the texts.

The Post Photographic Era

Photography today, depending on, among other things, technological developments, has a different appearance than earlier. As a basis for these texts, I have browsed literature that in one way or another has expressed ideas about photography or other images that have been possible to transfer into photographs. The idea was that in these writings I would find arguments for when / how the photographic image begins to be viewed as possible to be regarded as an independent art form. During the reading, however, I have realized that most of the authors in the sample concentrate on what is the difference between everyday photography and art photography. Therefore, this presentation will also address this difference. At the same time, we must keep in mind that many of the disciplines of art crossfertilize each other, so that what emerges as themes in literature, film, photography, music, sculpture or painting does not stay within the narrow niche where they are first presented. New technology also arouses curiosity in people who want to express themselves, which is obvious in terms of the use of film, video, audio recording or the use of digital software. The photographic image is no exception here. The digital development has at least led to that the technology for taking photographs, making film and music recordings of acceptable technical quality has then become affordable for many more than before.

The subtitle "The Post Photographic Era" on this collection of texts indicates that we are living in a time after the photographic era. Since the 1990s there have been descriptions of "the post-photographic era", among others by William J. Mitchell (1992) and Göran Sonesson (1999) whose thoughts are sometimes used in these texts. What is meant by "the post-photographic era"? Is it all about the transition from analogue to digital technology? Is it about the "magic" in film / photo allegedly disappearing in digital photography? Is it about the phenomenological notion that film and paper copies are objects as opposed to the digital file? The digital file does not, in a way, become an object until printing. The digital file can live its entire existence in digital form. Is the digital format really less of an object than the analog image? Can we imagine digital objects? The digital file has scope and mass - albeit in digital form on a hard drive or USB stick. Is there the same relationship between digital text and analog text in, for example, book or magazine form? Isn't the digital text contained in an e-book, for example, until it is read or printed? Is it a change in a clear technological sense or is it even something much bigger? Despite the argument about the "post-photographic era", we must admit that digital photography is also still about "writing with light".

The Western world sets the agenda for what photography is and is considered as. The western world gave birth to photography, nurtured it and established it worldwide, notes Nikos Panayotopoulos (2002:2). In fact, the photographic history of the West was established as the history of photography. The West has written "grammar" / syntax for international photography, set the framework for photographic production and evaluation in all other countries. The flow of the world's images is essentially unidirectional and the western world stands at the core of image production and distribution, making the concept of "history" a synonym for a post-constructed genealogy of itself. The semantic framework of the photographic medium – that is, the sum of the principles, rules and traditions – that emerged and developed in the industrialized Western world illustrates the Eurocentric nature of photography. In the colonial world, most of it was euro-centric – the English brought cricket and football as part of teaching the indigenous people of the colonies to become "Englishmen". The photograph followed in the footsteps of the colonial ambitions of the Western world.

We, according to some thinkers, are now living in the post photographic era, a relative of the postmodernist era. It also means that we live in an era that is the result of a long development of visual art. First came drawings, paintings, then came what we today call photographs. During the almost 200 years that we have lived with images made according to photographic methods since 1839 when Daguerre exposed his first image, photography has found its role in almost all communicative expressions in our society. When modern times have been going on for a while, some thinkers think that in order to describe contemporary times more accurately, we must have a new expression and new categories. We can assume that after the photographic era, we will step into, if we have not already done so, the post-photographic era, pending the next attempt of categorization. Is the post-photographic era about digital technology, then? With digital technology, many expressions converge to be found on the same website where we find texts, videos and photographs and they are available through the same type of reader, computer, cell phone or tablet. In that world, the effect becomes isolating and the behavior can be regarded as evasive if you are off grid. The question is whether this applies especially to photography.

We may see something similar on the way to take place, but we probably don't know what implications this will have on the future of photography. Already there are camera systems that can "tank" images of an entire city in the form of technology that Google, for example, uses to build two- and three-dimensional maps with street views around the world. Here we sometimes see real street photos of people eating ice cream or hugging each other.

What all this means is of course difficult to overlook, it is at best a divination about how digital technology might affect the photographic future. Already the way in which the photographic image may today be produced with computer assistance means that the camera has become a new tool, which does not require much effort and years of training to create decent photographs. Instead, we can put our power into enhancing our memories, our ideas about the stories that we are capturing and expressing in our world, as if we are strengthening our own bodies and beginning to resemble a cyborg with the digital camera technology to extend our own knowledge and capabilities. However, we do not yet have a camera in our body, but with the miniaturization that is going on we are on the right track. We can have so-called action cameras strapped to our bodies (or our bodies) and our clothes. The technology is used by some police forces to create summaries of events during police interventions. With further miniaturization, it soon becomes difficult to detect if someone is carrying a camera on their body which will eventually mean that we can make high-resolution photographs or video footage continuously on a stroll. When we get home, the imagery is just about ready to be distributed online.

Hardly visible cameras as a fairly integral part of our bodies: what can actually be more post-photographic than that? We know that images today are made to an extent that far exceeds the volume of images made in the 1950s. Is post-photographic about no longer "writing with light"? Probably not, we still command our surroundings to give us their stories and the surroundings do so with the help of light. The importance of the past may have to do with the fact that we are now not paying special attention to cameras because we know that there is a camera in every corner of our existence. It has become difficult to determine if we are "in the picture" and if we will see some "good images" filled with stories during the post-photographic era. The continuous photo shoots of our lives tend to be a contrast to traditional photography which has always been a snippet of reality.

Maybe the market for photographs will be saturated? Possibly if we argue about the careers for professional photographers, who already have a hard time creating their way of life. Of course, it is not possible to imagine that images would not be produced in the future. Interestingly, however, the right to make photographs in public places is under attack in the form of an EU proposal to prohibit photography of architecture, statues and "landmarks" that have an identifiable author in the form of an architect, artist or the like. The proposal is currently on the agenda in Sweden. It's all about what's in the back-drop as we walk through a city. It is an ominous sign of the times that the flow of images is likely to be restricted. One consideration is about the costs involved in controlling compliance with such prohibitions.

There are proposals for restrictions on the right to photograph in our surroundings. One example is Hungary, which has decided on severe restrictions. If we all get to photograph what we want, we will create stories all over the world. If a ban on some photography is introduced in the world we take for granted, we will surely land in the post-photography era. No one dares to make pictures in public space anymore, as it has become a criminal offense. What remains are images from the private sphere, which may not be as interesting as the one photographed in public space.

The reality in digital form

Are images of reality becoming different when they appear in digital form? This collection of texts will touch on these issues quite often. Partly because we have now lived with video and photos in digital form for a quarter of a century, and partly since many claim that digital has changed our view of images. The ongoing and probably not completed technology shift in the photographic image in the foreseeable future provides an opportunity to put questions about what happens to the content (meaning) as the technology that carries the content changes character. Many of the writers I rely on for the production of these texts can be called semiotics or phenomenologists. What, then, is semiotics and phenomenology? Semiotics (of Greek semeion: signs) is a collective name for theories and study of signs. *Semiotics* as science or discipline studies how meanings are perceived, and meaning is formed, in communicative situations, partly in the characters we use in written and spoken language, and in how they occur in other mediating resources such as gestures, images, physical things and biological processes. *Phenomenology* (of Greek phenomena, it seems) is a theory and method in philosophy, the doctrine of phenomena and being. In phenomenology, we study in particular the relationship between perception and the objects of perception, and seek to explain or describe ideas and beings to ourselves as they appear to us. Therefore, phenomenology does not primarily study causal relationships between objects.

Sarah J. Kember (2008: 175) argues that photography did not die the digital death that was perceived in the late 1900s. Rather, digitization has meant that today there is more of photography, possibly more types, than ever before. Kember believes that after 150 years we are not really sure what photography really is, the reason for this is partly due to the expansion of a limited range of disciplinary and conceptual frameworks. How much has the technology shift in photography affected the photographs and the experience of photographic images? The most important is probably the second part of the question: how will the shift in technology from analog to digital affect our experience of photography and thus the meaning we attribute to it? That is what we usually call a story in the image. If we do not allow a cultural expression such as photography the opportunity to carry content, or meaning, we will disqualify it as a cultural expression.

A new technology for imaging

According to history, the Stockholm exhibition 1866 became the beginning of photography in Sweden (Bremmer 2015:85-6). Photographer Johannes Jaeger had set up his camera equipment at one of the industrial hall stands to capture this scene. After a quick development and copying, the photograph is sent by horse to Ulriksdal's castle, where the bedridden monarch is allowed to watch the scene just an hour after it has taken place. The day after, the episode is recounted in the daily press, at the same time as the picture is for sale in the exhibition area. Jaeger's photography certainly sells a lot on its royal brilliance, but as surely as a picture of the exhibition experience itself. The camera has captured the Industrial Palace's characteristic "deceptive diversity" of people and objects, its abundance of objects.

At the Art and Industrial Exhibition in Stockholm in 1897, photography equipment was also shown and now came closer to the visitor, by making it possible to rent equipment. The media technologies presented to the audience at the exhibition in Stockholm – including the three "timewriters" phonograph, cinematographer and photography – were used at the same time to document and store the exhibition for the future (Ekström, Jülich & Snickars 2006:9). Of course, this was at a time when ordinary people did not have access to the camera. There were also restrictions on photography in the exhibition area for regular visitors. One type of camera that took "smaller" pictures was rented out by, among others, the photo company Sven Scholander. The cameras could expose 8x8, 9x12 or 12x16.5 cm images. The rent for the camera that took pictures in 8x8 cm format was SEK 35 (Ekström, Jülich & Snickars 2006: 10). A typographer at this time had a weekly salary of SEK 25-30 (Kommerskollegium 1903). We can probably assume that it was not the poorest citizens who rented cameras at the Art and Industrial Exhibition in 1897. When photography entered the public arena in the mid-1800s, it was, unsurprisingly, received with the way of thinking, writes the photography academic Victor Burgin (1982: 10). As far as the image is concerned, the criticism was about realism versus romance. The criticism of romantic philosophical foundations came from Auguste Comte's positivism. The intellect does not shape the external reality as Immanuel Kant saw it, but rather the objective world which must govern our thinking itself. To do that, we must accept that the reality we can see and touch is the only one that exists, writes Burgin. The romance, on the one hand, emphasized the author's preference: Delacroix writes in 1850 that painting is nothing more than a "sweeping reason", a bridge between the artist's mind and the spectator's. Realism, on the other hand, asserted the world's preeminence: according to Courbet, art painting can only portray "real and existing things", a unit that is abstract is not within the realm of the realm of painting. It seems that this discussion, according to Burgin (1982:10), was about the "content" of the image, what we might call meaning, message or "story". Realism was considered more true is the romantic portrayal of reality. We saw examples of feature films and fiction during the 1950s that formed the basis for the coinage of the concept of "sink realism". This "industrial" way of thinking about and accepting photography, which was a technical achievement among many others during the 19th century, was probably a usual manner of accepting new technology at this time.

The photographic image helps us to think. Slovenian researcher Ilija Tomanić Trivundža (2014: 217) agrees on the idea that photography, when it was invented during the first half of the 19th century, was conceived as a symbol of rational Western thinking and scientific methods for acquiring the world. By the early 1900s, photography had acquired a never-before-seen social status as a way of (visually) archiving, both as visual facts and in practice to visualise facts. The photograph managed to maintain this status until the early 2000s after weathering attacks on the ontological uncertainties brought about by the digital technology, which turned out to be more about the resurrection than the death of the media. In this simplified and widely accepted story, photography marches in line with modernity's project of Weberian disappointment around the world and seems to be an example of its "rationalisation and intellectualisation". Photography will thus be regarded as "*modern vision in every sense, but above all in its alliance with the vision of modern epistemology through its realism*". Photography plays its role well in documenting and discussing the modern world. Maybe this is about the seemingly realistic expression of photography. It is easy to "believe" that a photographic image is true, that is, depicts a moment that has taken place, which in turn represents a fragment of a time and a place.

The photograph does not stand alone in front of the viewer. Magnus Bremmer (2015: 17) argues that the history of photography is not merely the story of images. It is also a story of words. The contemporary audience's first photographic experience was rarely just photographic images, but instead the newly awakened reports and increasingly detailed testimonies in newspapers and magazines that spread around the world in 1839 after the daguerreotype was presented to the French Academy in January of that year. Once photographic images began to circulate in printed editions – first using manual reproduction techniques such as lithography, eventually as pasted paper copies – they were usually flanked by a descriptive, explanatory text. The presence of the printed word in the spread and consumption of photographic images in the 19th century is evident. Even today, it is routinely stated that "we rarely see a photograph that is not accompanied by words", as Victor Burgin emphasised. This shows that the idea of a photograph being able to stand on its own legs, without being accompanied by text does not really have a historical background.

Magnus Bremmer also thinks that photography was often praised for its detail in the beginning, but that this particular abundance of details was seen as a problem:

But critics also said that photographs showed too much, that they were too detailed. It was found that the mechanical imaging of photo technology made the image indistinguishable, that it could not distinguish the essential details from the essentials. Some thought that the photograph even distracted its viewers. What would you really look at? "The photograph abandons the eye". (Bremmer 2015:10).

Before the photograph, books and magazines were illustrated with different types of hand drawn images and the cartoonist could omit "irrelevant" details.

The argumentation about realism in art has its roots in a misunderstanding, argues André Bazin (1967:12). The conflict is based on a mix of the aesthetic and the psychological – between real realism, the need to give a valid expression to the world, both concrete and its essence – and the pseudo-realism of fraud aimed at deceiving the eye (or for that matter the mind). That is why medieval art never passed this crisis; at the same time vividly realistic and very spiritual, it knew nothing about the drama that was discovered as a result of technological development. Perspective was the sin of inheritance in Western painting. Now Bazin is a bit diligent, but his comments on the mix of aesthetic and psychological are interesting. The photographic image, even in the form of private photos, may seem to be loaded with a dynamic force that many thinkers have given up trying to explain. More about this in the section "Reading pictures".

What is photography – film or computer file?

In recent decades, photographers, as well as creators of other forms of media expression, have learned that digital technology is affecting the medium. The impact comes in different shapes. On the one hand, there is a speed in digital photography technology, which, for example, meets the media's demands for almost immediate publication on the web today, and on the other hand there are fears that the digital image is not as organic as traditional analog photography. Some reasoning is nostalgic, like using hand saws instead of electric saws when you're carpentering in the summer cottage. Other objections are about the expression. Can the digital image really convey the expression the authors are trying to put into it? The following texts are an attempt to give an orientation in how the thinking may go. At the same time, I should state that what is expressed here largely does so because it fits my view of the photographic image.

Canadian communication theorist Marshall McLuhan (1967:40) saw already in the 1960s how different media cooperate and together create something new: "no medium has any meaning or existence on its own, but only in constant interaction with other media." Perhaps we may sense this more clearly today when we see how digital technology has brought about a convergence of old media and also created media forms that did not exist before. It may rather be the case that old media is converted in accordance with current technology and developed starting with the old. A struggling cultural magazine that stops printing on paper and switches to online publishing may be an example.

However, there are things that mean that today it may be time to summarize thoughts about what photography is and does. We take photography so for granted today that it can be worthwhile to look back. We can, in thought, move back to the time when industrialism and modernism really had a firm grip on Western thinking. This means that the oldest writings here quoted were published in the 1920s.

When it comes to interpreting images or photographs, we may have become more blasé, but it is not at all certain that we even interpret pictures in a subjective way. It is possible that image interpretation is something we have learnt from the collective in which we live. People in other cultures may interpret images differently than the way we learn it in Europe, but for us, the European line of thought prevails.

Democratisation of the photographic image

The first thought is that it is only now, after the introduction of digital photo technology, that photography may be regarded as a democratic form of expression in the developed part of the world. In order to photograph, we must have access to the camera and today, even computer or mobile phone. However, we do not need to be a witch master in the analogue darkroom anymore, we can initially settle for simple image processing programs that are available to download for free from the Internet or accompany the camera when purchasing it. With image processing programs we can "improve" our images according to our individual taste. We do not need to stay in the dark yellow light of the analogue darkroom and become depressed by the lack of daylight. Today's development was predicted, among other things, by American futurist Alvin Toffler, who with another nomenclature in his "Future Schock: The Third Wave" from 1980 described the digitised network that connects us today.

Toffler's views were insightful, but we should not forget that others who said things about the future would have seemed at least as insightful if their predictions had come to fruition.

The digital evolution brings with it the thinking we have to learn to deal with. Australian cultural scientist Joanna Saasson (2007:299) has argued that through the direct conversion of light into a digital format, we create a stable image, which can be interpreted as photographs that exist only in digital form in a context that can be considered a true version of photography (writing with light) than those requiring the creation of a physical intermediary to display the image in material form. Even the idea that an original photograph has a unique value precisely "because of its status as a physical object" needs to be re-evaluated in the digital context. We have come to an intersection where we can make a digital copy of a digital copy with the push of a button, time and time again. In the end, they are all identical. In addition to all the copyright issues this entails, it may even mean that the old division into original and copy belongs to the past. Is the original the file that is on my hard drive or the copy that is on yours? The copyright means that it is mine being the original, because I made the picture, while your clone is a copy, even if it in essence, except the date, is the same as mine.

The cultural elite have always had a difficulty accepting "artistic" photographs as art. Pierre Bourdieu (1980:9) wrote in the 1960s about the class aspects of photography and believed that it is the vague notions of relationships within his own class and towards other classes that shape our image of photography. We express in the photographs we make our relationships with the immediate environment, while flirting with the ideas that exist about photography amongst the intellectual elite. It is in this way that members of photo clubs try to improve culturally by trying to refine photography and get a grip on the higher arts. The relationship between individuals and photographic methods is essentially a mediator relationship, since it always contains the reference to the relationship members of other social classes have with photography and thus to the whole structure of relations between classes. Bourdieu points to the populism in photography, while at the same time saying that the practice of photography is a way of approaching the intellectual elite. Where there is perhaps a driving force, even an amateur photographer with "reasonable" work effort can create a photograph that others may find exciting.

The American writer and filmmaker Susan Sontag (1973:8) also recognises that photography is not just the result of a meeting between an event and a photographer. Photography is an event in itself and one with increasingly compelling rights – to disturb, to invade or to ignore what is happening. Our comprehension of the situation is now articulated by the camera's interventions. The cameras present everywhere indicate that time is made up of interesting events, events that are worth photographing. This, in turn, makes it easy to feel that all events in progress, regardless of their moral character, should be allowed to complete themselves – so that something else can be brought into the world, namely photography. We wait for the event and make a picture. After the event has ended, the image will still exist and give the event a kind of immortality (and meaning) it would otherwise never have had. While real people are out there killing themselves or other real people, the photographer stays behind his camera, creating a small part of another world: the image world that will survive us all. The photographer creates a kind of legacy of time and events. If we use André Bazin's terminology then the time within the image will become embalmed.

More artistic photographs

The second thought is that this fairly recent real democratisation of photography is that more and more people are trying to create more artistic photographs. Digital technology and cheap modern cameras are so much more forgiving than analogue cameras in terms of technical knowledge.

One of a few questions one might ask is if the photographer is the images she creates? Why are there so many similar photographs? Maybe this is about learning to mimic a method. We want to be able to make photographs that are paraphrases of photographs that have made an impression on us. With mimicry as the only teacher, however, we risk preserving an aesthetics of images, which has already stagnated, in even harsher forms. Making a little more ambitious photographs may be about a way of expressing oneself, to refine some kind of meaning. Then photography becomes a kind of language. Like all other languages, we learn them by imitating. In the end, we may be able to express ourselves photographically.

Few of us acquire a language of their own – I speak an English that is a mishmash of American and British English, my French gets the French speakers to politely ask if I am Dutch. I imitate more or less well, but I have no English, no French, while I claim to have my own Swedish – where I may even vary the way of expression a lot more.

Photography as an art form

A third thought is that photography, almost 200 years after its emergence, is still often regarded as a kind of second rank art form. The French poet Charles Baudelaire, wrote in 1859 about photography:

"If photography is allowed to complement some of the functions of art, it will immediately nourish and destroy it, thanks to the natural alliance of photography with the mob. The photograph must therefore return to its proper task, which is to serve as a maid of science and art. " (reproduced in Benjamin 2008:294)

We notice a certain elitist view of the world, but it was also a different world from the one we live in about 150 years later. Baudelaire, however, let himself be delighted by the photographic image and it greatly contributed to his poetry. However, we see his approach to photography, it is not "real" art. We should not forget that those who at this time saw a photographic image were few, the photograph as a production form of images could still be said to be in its infancy.

Others saw the possibilities with the increasingly available photographic technology. The artist and photographer Man Ray (1974:71), who was deeply involved in photography during the early 1900s, talks about his view on photography in his autobiography:

"I had never shared the contempt other artists have shown for photography; there is no competition, rather the two media followed different paths. This was confirmed when I met prominent photographers, who were also painters and used the two means of expression at the same time without one intruding on the other. I admired and envied them."

Man Ray saw the possibilities of the photograph and did not care about the limitations or, rather tried to overcome them. Man Ray can thus be said to have been open-minded in his attitude towards photography.

The French semiotician Roland Barthes (1993:96) discusses the binary relationship between life and death in historical images. In every photograph depicting a person, death is always present. A photograph of a person tells the viewer both what is dead and what is to die in the future. This is what captures the viewer in the picture, what Barthes calls "Punctum". In particular, this may be clear when we consider an image of ourselves with one, or both, of our parents where we ourselves are in the image. At my age, parents are long gone and I can see in such a picture clearly who is next in line to be subject to death. The reason seems to be mainly that when I now consider the picture, I have access to facts.

The media historians Gitelman & Pingree (2004:xii) note that when new media emerge in a society, their place is initially poorly defined. The definitive meanings or functions of the new media are shaped over time by society's existing media habits, by common desires for new uses and by a slow process of adaptation between the two. It can probably also be said of digitalisation, which is a technological transformation that affects the media's production and distribution in a profound way. Although today we use photographs and its moving siblings, the film, in many contexts we may still not have seen the final use of the photograph. Can we guess what the actual use of photography looks like in the near future? Most who try to make predictions about the future fail. Some part of technological development is faster than others and we are experiencing technical opportunities that we could not foresee.

However, Alvin Toffler was already reasonably accurate in his vision for the future in 1980. Toffler predicted that we would be connected and share information, including photographs, with each other. Others, like IBM's chairman Thomas Watson, noted in 1943: *"I think there is a world market for maybe five computers."* However, Watson did not talk about personal computers and we should remember that it is all too easy to be wise when we have a proof in hand.

How then does participation in this interconnected internet work? What happens when amateurs and media companies meet? The Swedish media researcher Henrik Örnebring (2008:783) has studied what is called "user-generated" images in the daily newspapers' online editions. Örnebring believes that users, despite control attempts by owners, manage to create popular culturally oriented content and personal / everyday life-oriented content rather than news / information content. Direct user participation in news gathering, selection of news and news production is minimal and when it is available (as in the magazine's articles section), they are not displayed in the same way as material produced by the ordinary journalists. The only reader material that is given the same status as material produced by the news organisation itself is reader photos on news events. They are often followed by a "*PHOTO: Private*" byline. News / informative user content (mainly forum posts) is mainly produced in response to or in relation to material produced by the news organisation (ie user comments and discussion of published news). The user-generated content structures are provided by the newspapers rather than being "self-organising" and produced by the users themselves. Production is still centralised rather than distributed. What Örnebring addresses is one of the many results that digital technology has so far admitted.

It is also interesting that analog photography has not yet been completely replaced by digital. It may be due to (alleged) technical deficiencies in digital technology if the photographer has special requirements for images, but it can also be about the generation shift. The American media historians Gitelman & Pingree (2004:xiii) speak of the media in general when describing two trends as important. The first is the idea that each new media devours its predecessors, so that, for example, the printed book is doomed to leave room for digital texts. The second is the idea of transparency, that is, the newer a medium, the less it would affect the message. Here is a thought, which I believe indicates a belief that newer technology would be more perfect and thus not interfere with the possible message.

In this way, this newly gained transparency frees

information that was previously "stuck" in older technology. If we apply it to photography, we can imagine that the use of built-in light meters in the camera would have freed information, or at least made it easier for people other than professional photographers to make technically acceptable photos. With the software selection that also includes fairly cheap digital cameras and camera phones with automatic, the technology becomes even more transparent and makes it easier for ordinary people to make technically decent photos. Of course, for those who have learned the traditional technique, this is not "real" photography.

It is not clear whether the technology itself produces better information. It is probably true that today many more photographs are made every day than ever before. If photography is to mean anything to anyone other than the photographer and the closest circuit, more than just technology is required. What digital photography technology means may not yet, as Gitelman & Pingree (2004:xv) argue, has gotten its definitive meaning and its area of use determined by the public. This uncertain status of the digital photo may be what both attracts and repels users. One objection to the quality of digital photo technology is that only the number of users means that those who still consider it technically inferior to those who do not care, but use the technology as it is.

New media usually start as an imitation of something they replace, such as books that replace book scrolls and the Internet that have "pages" in analogy with the book, then perhaps they are established as something entirely their own. We have not yet seen the end of what digital technology can lead to that we still consider photography and film.

Although Gitelman & Pingtree is partly right in that new media devours its predecessors, old media lives by transferring concepts from the old technology to designate corresponding parts in the new. Maybe we can see how, with technical advances, we basically "modernise" the problems we have, we carry them with us into the new technologies.

Lisa Gitelman (2006: 6) argues that the defining scientific or obvious qualities of landscape photography have their background in eighteenth-century practice in terms of illustration and narrative as much as in any precision that is inherent in photographs unlike painted panoramas or other forms. The introduction of new media is never completely disruptive; it is, to a lesser extent, a theory of knowledge rupture than socially embedded places for ongoing negotiation of meaning as such. Comparing and contrasting new media thus offers a view of the negotiation as such – that is, of the disputed power conditions that determine the paths for new media to eventually become part of everyday life. Although the technology may seem to have a fast establishing phase, it does not happen overnight. Here, the development of technology has something in common with the "artistic" acceptance.

The slowing down of photography as an art form is a proven reality. Pierre Bourdieu (1990:7) pointed already in the 1960s out that some factor within the established society slows down the development of photography as an art form too much. While everything would lead one to expect this activity, which has no traditions and no requirements, to be turned over to individual anarchist improvisation, it instead suggests that there is nothing more regulated and conventional than photographic methods and amateur photographs – on occasion that give rise to photography, such as objects, places and people photographed or the actual composition of the images, everything seems to follow an implied canon that is commonly imposed and which informed amateurs or aesthetics note as such, only to condemn them as examples of bad taste or technical clumsiness. If, in these stylish, rigid, crisscrossed photographs, made in accordance with a social label that produces photographs of family parties and "holiday memories," we have not been able to identify which implicit or explicit rules define its aesthetics, it is probably because we have interrupted an overly limited (and socially shaped) definition of cultural legitimacy. Unlike fully accepted artistic activities, such as painting or music, photographic practice is something that is considered accessible to everyone, from both technical and financial points of view. Participants do not feel that they are being measured against an explicit and codified system that defines legitimate practice in terms of its objects, both from a technical and economic point of view, hence the analysis of the subjective or objective meaning that subjects provide photography as a practice or as a cultural one. Work that seizes the aesthetics (and ethics) of different groups or classes, and especially the popular "aesthetics", which is exceptionally manifested in it, Bourdieu argues. In principle, Bourdieu states that there are those who are subject to photographic practice, and those who are not.

Is the individual photograph an independent object com-

compared to a book, a bicycle or a pen? Victor Burgin (1982:11) believes that photography did not really follow the expected development of a new art form. During the development we now know as "modernism", the sign would be completely erased from the surface. The work of art would become a completely independent material object that made no reference to anything outside its own boundaries. The surface itself – its color, its texture, its edge – would be the only content of the work. After cubism, modernism would free art from its old compulsion to represent, but it was about representation on the terms that cubism itself had criticised: illusion and communication. However, the photograph was not capable of following the painterly art of modernist abstraction without appearing to be seeking effect. The unprecedented capacity that photography had for similarities seemed most appropriate to determine its specific tasks and to separate photography from painting. Sure, during the modern period, a form of "photographic modernism" has emerged based on different concepts of "photographic vision", but it has been a weak and uncertain purchase of the considerations of "content" which remains so stubbornly central to our photographic experience. Is the photograph at all capable of freeing itself from the "reality" that a photograph usually emanates from?

If we compare the photograph with painted art, some writers trace some differences between the two. Australian architect William J. Mitchell (1992:29) argues along the line that a photograph is a photograph *of* something, while a painting need not be an image of something existing. This means that although angels do not exist, it is possible to paint an angel, but it is difficult to make a photograph of one. Similarly, it is possible to paint a horse that is not a specific horse, but it is impossible to make a photograph of a horse that is not a specific horse. According to this view, photography would be ill-suited for general expressions and more suitable for specific images, for example of a very specific horse.

As far as this content is concerned, our way of perceiving photography to a very large extent has not yet managed to break away from the gravitational field of eighteenth-century thinking. It is a thinking that is dominated by a metaphor of depth where the surface of the photograph is regarded as a projection of something that lies "behind" or "beyond" the surface, where the snippet of the photograph marks the entrance to something more profound, "reality" itself, the artist's "expression" or both. However, the surface of the photograph hides nothing but its own superficiality. Whatever meanings and powers we can build upon its prompting can not come to some final conclusion. They can not be maintained long in the imaginary convergence points where the experience of a writer or the truth of a reality lies, Victor Burgin (1982:11) points out.

William J. Mitchell (1992:49) too argues that digital photography is problematic since there is not a unique negative as in the case of the analogue film. A digital image file can be copied endlessly without loss of quality. The only thing that separates the copy from the original is the date in the file. The original file can be deleted, but all of its potential clones can live. Digital images can also be rendered from databases, which means that we have to ask whether the database is the original or the originator? Mitchell believes copyright law has a lot to work with. The Bern Convention of copyright today speaks about copyright on works that are: "fixed in some tangible medium of expression".

How did all these notions come about that the more mechanised image is not art? Of course, we can award all working hours spent on a work of art. It is a way of valuing art. Another is to award the "charge", the expression, the meaning, which the current work of art manages to convey. This is not primarily about the task of the artwork, but about what the viewer manages to extract from the artwork.

The artist's work is thus merely a raw material for the experience created by the viewer. Perhaps it is presumptuous, or even counterproductive, to view the art experience in this way. Without a viewer, however, neither a painting nor a photograph can be said to fulfill its ultimate function. By analogy with the "tree that falls in the forest" is a photograph that no one sees more than the creation of a kind of limbo, which questions its existence.

As long as it is about some kind of visual art, which can be more or less depictive, it seems that what the visual is about what is decided by the viewer. How, where and in what way is the artist in this way of looking at the artwork? The artist has a role, but that role is also determined by the viewer, who is the one who "interprets" what the artist has managed to achieve.

Do I mean that we should stop worshiping the author and instead concentrate on the more offensive role of the viewer? To some degree, I see that the most important person is the viewer. It is kind of in the same vein as when we ask if it is the winner or who comes second who is most important in sports competitions. If there were not two participants, there would be no winner, but only one performer. If there were no viewers, there would also be no works of art. Or do we find it difficult today to distinguish between photographic "drafts" and "published" works. We store the digital images on any type of hard drive that is not readable to the naked eye; we must have a computer or tablet to study the photographs. It always raises the question of when the photograph actually is created. Isn't it enough to have a digital file on a hard drive? Is a printout of the digital file required in a medium reminiscent of an image produced with a traditional analog magnifier so that the image becomes more material, tangible? Or is it enough that the image exists as a digital file for us to recognise it as a photograph? French cultural anthropologist Bruno Latour (1993:10), who criticised the concept of "modernism", saying that what we call "modernity" exists in as many versions as there are thinkers or journalists, but all their definitions point back in one way or another. towards the time elapsed. The adjective "modern" denotes a new order, an acceleration, a break, a revolution in time. When the some of the words "modern", "modernisation", or "modernity" comes up in the conversation, by this we define an age-old and stable past. In addition, the word is always thrown into the middle of a fight, in a quarrel where there are winners and losers, the old and the modernists.

"Modernity" is thus doubly asymmetrical: it discerns an interruption in the course of ordinary times and a battle in which there are the winners and the defeated. So many of our contemporaries are reluctant to use this adjective today.

If we qualify it with prepositions, it is because we feel less confident in our ability to assert this dual asymmetry: we can no longer point to the irreversible arrow of time, not nor can we award prizes to the winners. In the countless quarrels between the old and the modernists, the former emerge as winners as often as the latter, and we cannot say whether revolutions end the old regimes or bring them to fruition. Hence that scepticism, Bruno Latour notes, which, strangely enough, is called the "post" modern, even though we do not know whether it is capable of taking over from modernism.

Can this reasoning be transferred to the boundary between the photographic and the post-photographic era? Is post-photographic about whether we can distinguish a distance from the photographic? What happens to the person who does not understand what is happening? Can we interpret images in established ways for centuries without changing to the slightest extent to the interpretations of the digital world? On the one hand, of course, aesthetic ideas apply even if the technology changes, but on the other hand, the aesthetics ought to be influenced by the technology shift.

Photography: documentation or art form?

Is photography always about just pressing the shutter button and "making a snapshot"? How do you load a photographic image with content and let it become a work of art? Is there a creative moment when a photographic image is created? Many "art photographers" probably want to claim that. Photography has since the childhood of photographic technology in the early 1800s been discussed in terms of "originality", that is, when a photograph transitions from being pure documentation, a depiction of the physical world, at a certain point in time that all viewers can approve as "faithful to the reality", to be a work of art that is judged in different ways depending on the viewer's connotations. Pierre Bourdieu (1990:74) argues that the view of photography as a perfectly realistic and objective record of the visible world is about the fact that photography is assigned the social use of being "realistic" and "objective". Adhering to this way of looking at photography, the use of photography by military, police, doctors and press has been the idea. If there are pictures of the hit, crime or injury then the photograph "objectively" shows what it looked like when it happened. Here it is thus about the photographic image as documentation.

The meaning of the photographic image

Photo documents may touch, have a meaning, but many

see it as if only 'art' can touch – it has meaning and can convey something.

In that case, the photograph that touches, conveying meaning could be regarded as art. Bourdieu (1995) uses the concept 'social capital' that deals with the social contacts and networks with which a person interacts. I imagine photographers are part of social networks for their production of photographs of their culture. In the social space with which Bourdieu resembles society, there are countless social fields. A field is populated by a defined group of individuals or agents. In order to be perceived as a social field, this field must adopt specific features which in some way make it indistinguishable.

The agents in the same field are united in, for example, a common interest, a common cultural position or similar economic status. A field is thus not an autonomous phenomenon in itself and does not exist independently of human coexistence. Bourdieu's field, says Donald Broady (1998:15), if we seek a definition that is as general as possible, can be defined as a system of relations between positions. By social field (also called battle field or competition field), Bourdieu refers to a changing area in society where people and institutions are pursuing something that is common to them. Within the field of education science, for example, the school's goals and meaning are contested.

Bourdieu distinguishes between, on the one hand, production fields, populated by specialists who create ideas and values, and on the other, consumption fields.

Jean Baudrillard (2009:52) argues that it is little added to attribute the photographic image meaning. By doing so, you create motives that pose. The objects themselves begin to pose in the light of meaning as soon as they feel a glance. I think of some of our younger citizens who do a duck-face as soon as a camera shows up near them.

Theodor Adorno (1991:73, 93), in his articles from the 1970s, strongly criticises the cultural industry he encountered in especially the United States. Adorno mainly see a lack a conflict in the cultural products produced and he accuses the cultural monopoly for this development. Adorno sees a pastime, filled with emptiness. Adorno is even more dismayed by the texts that the cultural industry produces – he sees texts as the academic he is: photographs, movies, soap operas or other entertainment is text. The authentic images on the movie screen as well as the non-authentic ones encountered in the lyrics of hit songs where the worn phrases appear so rigidly and so often that their original meaning is lost and we hear them only as repetitions whose smoothness always stands for the one and same meaning. Adorno delivers a devastating critique of the cultural industry where emptiness, in his view, replaces content and meaning. His comrade from the Frankfurt School, Walter Benjamin, also realised that popular culture or mass culture lost something when exclusivity turned into mass production.

Walter Benjamin (2008 and 1936:21) writes as early as 1936 about the reproducibility of a work of art as problematic. Artwork has been possible to multiply since centuries through woodcuts and lithographic printing, but Benjamin believes that even in the most perfect reproduction, one thing is missing: here and now – the unique work of the artwork in a certain place. The photograph became affordable in the late 1800s becoming relatively inexpensive. In this regard, photography is a child of the general and increasingly flow of commodity production that has emerged through industrialism. This would mean that photography loses the "aura" that Benjamin calls "here and now", but if the photograph is not considered a work of art, it has no aura to lose. Benjamin believes that mass reproduction of art, especially within photography and film, could meet the demands of a new, revolutionary art policy. In extension to the price of the unique, the "aura", moved away from the main room and replaced with mass editions. This event changes the tradition and is closely associated with the mass movements of the 1930s, whose most powerful tool is the film. Benjamin believed that during the 1930s, as a result of mass media editions, changes in human perception occurred that could be interpreted as the decay of auras. This meant that the uniqueness of a work of art disappeared, but Benjamin says, the work of art had the potential to become political by allowing it to be owned by everyone through mass reproduction.

Jean Baudrillard (1983:98-100) points out that Walter Benjamin found that reproduction absorbs the production process. Benjamin saw this happening in art, film and photography as this opened up new areas without classical productivity. Baudrillard believes that today we know that all material production (fashion, media, advertising, information and communication networks) is going through this phase. Benjamin first (and later McLuhan) did not view technology as a "production force" (where Marxist analysis is locked) but as a medium, as the form and principle of a whole new generation of reason. The mere fact that something can simply be reproduced, in duplicate, is already a revolution; you only have to take into account the shock when people not accustomed to moden technology see, for the very first time, two identical books. That these two technical products should correspond under the sign of socially necessary work is less important in the long run than the series of repetition of the same object (some of which are also individuals as labor). Technology as a medium not only dominates the "message" of the product (utility value), but also the labor that Marx wanted to make to the revolutionary message of production. Benjamin and McLuhan saw the issue more clearly than Marx; they saw its true message: the ultimatum lay in reproduction itself. And that production no longer has any meaning; its social finality is lost in the series. Simulacra wins over history.

The American writer and filmmaker Susan Sontag (1973:21) argues almost 40 years after Benjamin that photography has become a pastime, almost as common as "sex and dancing". Sontag concludes that most do not practice photography as an art form, but rather as a social rite, an anxiety suppressor and a means of power. The difference between the time Benjamin describes and Sontag's era is about as long as up to our present time. Sontag's description of general photography is even more true today, where we are all a kind of "one-man editorial desk" who can post material on social media in a completely different way than 40 or 80 years ago.

Sontag also believes that traditional art rests on the distinction between authenticity and falsity, between original and copy, between good taste and bad taste. Media are blurring these boundaries.

The traditional art assumes that certain experiences or subjects have meaning and that the traditional media are in principle contentless. Sontag (1973:117) refers to Marshal McLuhan's thesis that the medium is the message. Sontag predicts that art will increasingly have photography as the norm.

Photography does not threaten the art of painting

The photograph did not emerge to function as a challenge to the traditional visual arts, says Jean-Francois Lyotard (1984:74). The threat was no greater than what the feature movie delivered against the narrative book art. Lyotard is of the opinion that mechanical or industrial compensation does not in itself constitute a disaster. At least if one does not believe that art in its essence is an expression of an individual genius in combination with craftsmanship at the elite level.

Art painting has never imagined the "snapshot" of photography, writes Jean-Luc Nancy (2005:104), where an "I" with one click meets with a "You", another "I". Nancy thinks this is about a common experience with the support of analogue or digital technique, the eye and light, a view from the outside and one from the inside, the special gaze (active) and the other (passive). Nancy thinks that photography is a monster with two subjects, with a double human body and a lonely empty head whose single eye flashes "on" and "off". Does the "meaning" of this snapshot arise in the "togetherness" that the photographer and the photographee can possibly experience? Ever since the photo is made they are in a way connected, they have a common experience, which is also perpetuated on film or memory card.

Roland Barthes (1993:32-34) argues that photography is a kind of primitive theater, a kind of 'Tableau vivant', a kind of motionless and painted face behind which we see death. Barthes calls the photographer the Operator, whose job it is to "shock" the subject by: making images without previous warning, rare pictures, caught in flight, with technical skill (blur) or found subject (trouvaille). Photography, to surprise, photograph what is worth noting, but eventually everything that was previously photographed is worth noting. Thus, appearances and objects are elevated by exposure to photography.

This is an interesting observation, which may be led into evidence. There may be an agenda for what is photographable during certain time periods until someone begins to photograph other subjects. Barthes (1993:38) also claims that photography is subversive, not because of the surprises or the technical brilliance, but especially when it "thinks". I imagine that with this Barthes suggests that the photograph has a message, or meaning, for the individual viewer. However, this does not mean that all viewers experience the same meaning.

Roland Barthes presents the two concepts "studium" and "punctum" as a means of interpreting photographs and describing what captures the viewer's attention. Barthes is primarily looking for what photographs may tell, but photographs are material objects of the special character that they "represent" something. "studium", according to Barthes, represents an extension of the image in the room

– a field that the viewer, with the help of his knowledge and cultural luggage, perceives as something quite familiar. Barthes believes that it is a kind of acquired recognition. This "studium" allows the viewer to function as part of what the image represents – including both facial expressions, gestures, surroundings and actions. Some of this reasoning leads in the direction that we can not see and understand what we have not already seen. Our cultural heritage in the ethnological sense gives us the meaning, which is thus not in the picture, it first arises in our brain. We cannot understand what lies outside our frame of reference. By extension, it could explain why pioneering visual artists find it difficult to, at first, have their art accepted by viewers. Viewers simply do not have the tools to understand what these pioneering artists want. The often cited concept of "punctum" stands for a disturbance, or a beat mark, in "studium". "Punctum" stands for the content that protrudes from the image, such as a scar or a cut. It is the chance that a dice throw hits the viewer. Barthes (1993:25 ff) argues that "studium" and "punctum" represent two themes in the photographic image. Barthes does not find "punctum" in all images – many of the images he looks at only arouse a general and polite interest. Barthes believes that these do not contain any "punctum". They may or may not appeal to him, but without touching him. These pictures are the subject of a pure ”studium".

Jean-Paul Sartre (2005:25) describes how he makes a photograph of a friend to enhance the imaginary image of the friend he carries within himself. Although it is an excellent image of the friend it lacks life, but it certainly gives the friend's features. Sartre (2005:17) complements by looking at a cartoon a famous cartoonist made of his friend and this is inspired by the fact that some features are distorted now giving him back his picture of the friend. Sartre also agues that when we view an image, we animate it, and we are aware that we give the image life. We borrow that life. This is reminiscent of Barthes 'Punctum' which is the content of an image that makes it interesting to the viewer. Now Sartre looks at a picture of his friend and gets closer to the memory of his friend. The question is what does this picture tell someone else, someone unfamiliar with that friend?

Ansel Adams (1981:12), who was an practicing photographer, describes the technical prerequisites for photography in a way that almost leads to the viewer. Adams explains the visualisation concept his photography is based on a creative and subjective way of approaching his photography. Visualisation helps the photographer to project the final image in the mind before the photographer begins to photograph. Adams is convinced that "the best" photographers see the image in front of them, either through a conscious strategy or through some kind of intuitive emotion. This is similar to the stories that exist about sculptors who just want to chop away what is hiding the figure found in wood or marble.

If we leave the professional photographer for a while, Henri Lefevre argues that leisure activities at the highest level create active approaches, highly specialised jobs, linked to technology and thus comprising a technical element independent of professional specialisation. Digital cameras are often equipped with program choices, which means that photography, as an act, is really just pressing the button. The amateur photographer can choose to concentrate on the subject. Lefebvre (1991:32) points to photography as such an occupation. According to Lefebvre, photography is an activity that is closely related to technological development. Today, everyone, including the professional photographers, makes far more pictures than just a few decades ago. So far, Lefebvre has a point in that technological development enables a wider way of photographers. Digital cameras also have far greater exposure ranges than analog cameras, which simplifies photography.

The average photographer, says Bourdieu (1990:75), takes the world as he or she sees it, with a logic that borrows its categories from ancient art. Images that deviate from the usual norm are astonishing. Popular photography has a time dimension in that it takes a snippet of everyday perception and creates endless series of images, dream images, with figures, frozen in the moment and it is thus that photography loses its opportunity to really affect. This is, according to Bourdieu, the true paradox of photography. Is it then the number of images, the voluminous flow, that reduces the possibility of affecting? Bourdieu may be on the track of something, there is undeniably a risk that we will be blunted when we are exposed to far more impressions than we are used to experiencing.

W.J.T. Mitchell (2005:76) describes the image as always provided with a material being, it is always carried by a medium which is material. These substrates may be magazines, books, posters or films. The image has a tendency to travel between different media. We may consider objects in our environment – from diminutive material cultural products such as the stapler on the desk to a shopping center – which can also be seen as a material cultural product, albeit composed of a number of disparate parts. Mitchell puts the question what happens to an image when it is subject to over- and underestimation, when it has some kind of "added value". Mitchell is trying to figure out how images achieve values that are not in proportion to their actual weight and what critical practice is required to create a valid image evaluation. This goes on, according to Mitchell, in our time, which is played out after the "visual turn" that has created new or drawn attention to pre-existing problems regarding how we view images and evaluate them. (In the later decades of the 20th century, scholars within the humanities and social sciences began to study social phenomena, taking into account, inter alia, the narrative, visual or material. The shifts between these approaches are referred to as "turns". Mitchell's reasoning about added value, I think, may be described as the charge or meaning a photographic image can get, without that it to the outside seems to deserve it. The photograph may appear technically inferior, may be blurry, it is difficult to determine what it represents, but it is perhaps this that initiates reactions to the material in our brains, the viewer posts a personal meaning, like Barthes 'punctum' and the image gets a life that maybe only one viewer sees, while everyone else is questioning this alleged charge of the image.

Photographs that get better over time

In my photo archive I have some black and white photos from the early 1970s, they represent a friend who died about ten years after the images were made. When I checked my contact sheets last summer, I thought she looked so sad in the pictures. (Contact sheets are made by putting the developed film on a photo paper and highlighting it. You get positive images on a scale of 1: 1 of the negatives.) While my friend was still alive, they were pictures of a friend, without the emotional charge that her passing and the past few years put in these images for me. The contact sheets are today really in tune with Bourdieu's reasoning, about 'frozen moments'. For those who did not know this woman, they may be a time document, which we can all watch depending on the attire and surroundings, but for those of us who know her fate, the pictures are more than just frozen moments. Maybe I remember my friend better by looking at the photos that represent her, like Sartre when he looks at the photo of his friend and needs a drawing to remember him more clearly. I load those images with a meaning that does not seem to exist for any other viewer.

When I return to my negative albums from the 1960s and 1970s, I am surprised to discover what negatives I never chose to copy then. My views on images have undoubtedly changed over the decades that have passed since then. The photographs, of course, have not objectively become "better", but rather my changed view of them is that I have changed myself over the decades that have passed. This means that I can look at the images I made in my teens in a whole new way. I see things in them I didn't discover then. That probably means they tell me something completely different to me today than they did 40 or 50 years ago.

The question is whether those images can be considered "better" or if it is as if I am a whole different viewer today, after all these years? In many ways I am different, but at the same time I am still that teenager. But, with layers upon layers of experience in managing images, both in business and in private, it is of course another viewer who now regards the images in those negative albums.

At the same time, I'm not so keen on doing the job of scanning the negatives and transporting the images into the present since what is considered in those images is probably another story belonging to another viewer. The absurd thing is that the viewer is me at the same time as he is not. It's all the years that separate us.

Even my sister and childhood friends have a hard time recognising the stories I see in those old photographs. I am another person, the images are loaded with memories that are so far back that I am surprised that we even have anything to remember from that time.

It does not have to be real memories. Somehow I might fabricate them to give myself an experience of the old negatives. Whatever the case, I am primarily interested in how my view over time is filled with new content, new reactions and new reflections in front of an image that I once considered without special interest. This is an example of episodic evidence of an aspect that our relationship with photographs is not static, but is shifted over time. It would be strange otherwise, since most things seem to change over time.

Since it is my life experience that has been included in the equation with the old negatives, this presumedly means that all my old photographic images would probably have undergone the same metamorphosis when I look at them. What it means for my experience of them is that I marvel at them as new, even though I viewed the negatives 40 years ago. In addition, my thoughts are on how I would have made the corresponding photographs today, if I had at all endeavored to make them. Maybe today I would choose other motifs, other compositions and other sections of reality? It is difficult to determine which of the above concepts would have been most pervasive for the recreation of the old photographs today.

What I care most about though is that I somehow find myself thinking that these old images would be of interest to me later in life – like in the present. Of course, what this interest would look like, I couldn't imagine. There was just a belief that these pictures and texts I produced should be saved. Some have come into use in various projects, others are still waiting to be brought into use again. Maybe I can, maybe not.

Gilles Deleuze (1986:24) writes mainly about movies, but has some reflections on the individual pictures or scenes. Deleuze believes that photography is a kind of "molding" where the form organises the object's internal forces in such a way that they reach a kind of equilibrium position at a certain point (immobile section). However, this organisation does not stop when the equilibrium is reached and continues to change the mold continuously, thus creating a variable, uninterrupted temporary mold. In the movies, this happens 24 times a second, while with a still camera, even if we expose still images in sequence (motor) usually land at a maximum of 14 frames per second. The still photographer then selects one of these temporary images to convey the expression alone he / she wants to convey.

Photography that touches, conveys meaning, may be regarded as art. A documentary photo, made by a police investigator or a doctor to document a crime or injury, definitely conveys meaning as a document and can also convey meaning beyond its role as a document.

Bourdieu believes that the field (here interpreted as meaning) is based on the fact that there are participants with essentially the same orientation. They are the ones that make up the field. Bourdieu (1992:82) argues that for those who are completely out of the game, it is difficult to understand the efforts made in the future and prestige during the course of the game. For the viewer of the final photographs, according to this way of regarding them, only those who themselves try to make similar photographs would really understand what meaning they carry.

Not simular meaning

Let's return to Roland Barthes's (1993:25 ff) ideas about "Punctum" and "Studium". "Punctum" stands for a disturbance, or a mark, in "Studium". "Punctum" stands for the content of what protrudes from the image, such as a scar or a mismatch. There is the chance that a dice throw hits the viewer. Barthes thinks that "Studium" and "Punctum" represent two themes in the photographic image. Among other things, Barthes believes that what is outside the viewer's frame of reference cannot be understood. What is meaningful to one individual may not be that to the other. An example of this is to consider match images from judo competitions. Although I have spent over 30 years in the judo world, I realise that what I see / discover in a photo in the form of meaning is something quite different from what a novice in judo discovers in the image. We have two separate "Punctum" or variants of the individual meaning we find in the picture.

Finally, when we can put the label "art" in a photograph, it is about a high-level photograph that can be said to reach a plateau where the photograph gives something more than what is objectively in the image. Mitchell's (2005:76) idea of a kind of "added value" in the picture is similar to Barthes' idea of "Punctum", but also related to Walter Benjamin's (2008:21) idea that reproduction causes the aura of the image to diminish in value. We can with difficulty specify the subset of a photograph that "raises" it from documentation to art. Perhaps the charm of looking at photographic images is that it is not easy to decide where, on a given scale, we should rank them. Maybe it is enough that the image gives us, as viewers, a meaning in our present time?

As early as the 1960s, Bourdieu (1990:112) wrote that photography as a work of art was difficult to separate from the fact that photographs are made with a machine (camera) and that photographs are also made by others beside those aspiring to make art. It is about ordinary people and that meant that photography could be considered "vulgar", at least in meritocratic France. Perhaps it is this dual vision and practice of photography that creates problems. A type of problem that is not as clear as in older art forms like art painting or music. On closer reflection, even these modes of expression have undergone a revolution in the digital era. Now bands (DJs) are performing on stage and presenting pre-recorded digital audio files. If we judge the meaning of these concerts according to the effect they have on the audience, it is art. Many individuals feel that they are affected and have some kind of meaning conveyed to them.

If the meaning, or message, in a photograph is what matters, all images we are touched by, whether made by recognised art photographers, or by some relative, should be classified as art. The question is perhaps whether what in society's opinion is called art requires that more than one individual perceives it as art. However, that discussion is beyond this text.

The Peculiarities of the Photographic Image

What can the photographic image give the viewer that no other visual art forms are capable of? What exactly does the photographic image give us viewers? Can we trace any kind of dialogue between the viewer and the photograph? W. J. T. Mitchell (1996) puts the question when he formulates it as: *"What do pictures really want?"* Mitchell's idea is that this question should give us a new and different view of the inherant power and meaning of the image. In addition, his question is about what values we assign to an image. It may even be about what we allow the image to do with us, how it affects us. We may not even see that the image is something different from our own existence? May the image contain a meaning different from the one we already are used to?

Phenomenological thoughts that encompass objects that affect us through their mere presence have origins that go way back. The question is whether the production of objects by the analog photographic technology has been reduced by digital technology. In the digital form, the photographic image has no distribution in the room and is not an object in the traditional sense. We can't really read (see) the digital image without the help of a digital reader in the form of a computer, tablet or cell phone. Many will agree that images in general, including photographs, affect us. They "tell us" something. The question is whether the photographic images say something else if they exist in digital form, compared to the traditional analog form of silver emulsion on glass or film substrate.

What, then, does the photographic image contain that makes it so exciting for us viewers? Teodora Cosman (2012:269), among others, explains how the photographic image contains two elements that are fundamental to its description and function. The first is light (or its opposite and its absence: shadow and darkness) that can lead us to its metaphysics and the metaphors for mysticism and revelation. The other important element is the act of writing, tracing, the visible mark of *graphein* or signing, printing, sculpting in depth! Tupos: imprint gestures that include intimate contact with support as well as with the object whose traces remain visible. Therefore, in the case of the "dematerialised" images of today, we always feel compelled to make the distinction "digital" or "analog" to clarify what kind of photography we are talking about. Does this mean that something significant has changed in our understanding of this phenomenon, that the name of photography, "writing with light" does not quite correspond to the way digital images appear. Cosman quotes André Rouille:

"La mal nommée photographie numerique n'est en aucun cas une declinaison numérique de la photographie. Une rupture radicale les sépare: leur diffèrence n'est pas de degré mais de nature." (The naming of digital photography is by no means a misnomer of digital photography. A radical breakup separates them: the difference is not in degree but in kind.)

How this distinction manages to survive can still be said

to be shrouded in obscurity. The literary handling of images is, of course, rather unconvincing in its tribute to the images' somewhat eerie personality, writes Mitchell (1996). Magical portraits, masks and mirrors, living statues and haunted houses are everywhere in both modern and traditional stories and the aura of these imaginary images seeps both professional and popular attitudes into real images. By photographing motifs that are already filled with mysticism and magic, do we want to load the photograph with further meaning? Maybe to the level of parody. Art scholars may "know" that the images they study are only material objects coated in colors and shapes, but often they talk and act as if the images had a will, consciousness, agency and desire. The images in this way become co-players in our lives, perhaps not only when we study the images.

Do we allow the images to affect us or is it the case that we have no choice? Everyone knows that a photograph of their mother is not alive, but they will still be reluctant to disfigure or destroy it, Mitchell notes. No modern, rational, secular person thinks that images should be treated as people, but we always seem to be prepared to make exceptions for special cases. An image can follow us through life in the form of a portrait photo in the wallet or as a digital image in our cell phone. As a desktop image in my computers, I keep a photo of myself as an eighteen year old in order not to forget the dreams I once had. I, as an eighteen-year-old, consider the considerably older man I have grown into. At the same time, I see the image of myself as an eighteen-year-old.

It is not difficult to show that the idea of personality in

images is as vivid in the modern world as it was in historical societies. Are those images meant to be loaded, artistic or what you want them to be, something that exists freely without the image really having anything to do with the essence of the image itself? Is the content available even before the photograph was made?

The difficulty is knowing what to say next, says Mitchell (1996). How are traditional attitudes recycled into images such as idolatry, fetishism or totemism in modern societies? Is it the job of the cultural critic to demystify these images, to crush the modern idols, to reveal the fetishes that enslave people? Is it to distinguish between true and false, healthy and sick, pure and unclean, good and evil images? Are the images the area where political struggle should be waged, the place where a new ethic should be articulated? Do we today let the pictures speak to us in a way that we can no longer defend ourselves against?

We can put all these questions and many more, but are we as viewers willing to deal with the images and analyse their role in our lives? We, who are now living in the western world, are probably the most exposed and long-lived population using man-made images of all the people that ever lived. What does this mean for our relationship with images in all forms? Do they speak to us and if so, what do they want? It is interesting that we let images, or their materiality, agents or whatever, affect us fairly regularly.

We guard ourselves against "false prophets," that is, people who try to change our minds – political or religious. Do we defend ourselves in the same way against the universal messages that images bombard us with? Are we able to defend ourselves?

Is this stream of thoughts and ideas inherent in the man-made images that modern society is about?

What kind of reality are we talking about? Walter Benjamin, one of the thinkers of the Frankfurt School, wrote a lot about the media and even photography in the 1920s and 30s. Benjamin (2008:277-279) argued that it is a matter of the camera seeing a different reality compared to that of the eye. It is different, in particular, in that the field of view fulfilled by human consciousness is replaced by an unconscious human field of view. So, although we usually understand how people walk, if only in broad terms, we probably know nothing about what they look like in the fraction of a second when a step begins. The photographic image and its aids, slow motion captures and magnifications, provide information on this. Only on this path does one get to know about the optically-unconscious, as well as about the operational-unconscious through psychoanalysis. Benjamin was fascinated by how photography could show structures in nature that were difficult to see with the naked human eye.

It is also about WHEN we look at a picture. I notice that when I look at negatives that are 40 years old, there are other images than the ones I made enlargements of that are interesting now. It may be that on a different negative than the one I long time ago did a a copy of there is more visible background, more of the environment the picture is made in, or a different angle of the people who appear in the image. My perspective on the images may have gone from seeing the images as snapshots from yesterday to looking at them with heavily nostalgic approaches – the environment and the people I once knew. They have become my "embalmed time". In some cases, neither the people nor the environment are left any longer. Does this mean that we are not on our guard against the images?

Jean Baudrillard (1983:120) describes an exciting view of photography and images in general. Every image, every media message, including all functional environmental objects, is a test – that is, in the term's complete, liberating response mechanisms without stereotypes and analytical models, Baudrillard notes. Today, the motifs are no longer "functional" in the traditional sense of the word. No reservations, they test you. It has nothing to do with the object of yesteryear, nothing more than media news with a "reality" of facts. Both motifs and information are already the result of a selection, a montage, a perspective. They have already tested "reality" and have only asked questions that "answered back" to them. They have broken down the reality into simple elements that they have rebuilt in the scenarios of regulated opposition, just as the photographers sets their contrasts, lights and angles on their subject (any photographer will tell you: you can do anything, all you have to do is approach the object from the right angle at the right moment or mood that will give the right answer to the instantaneous test of the instrument and its code). Is it just about attitudes and technology?

It is just like the test or referendum when translating a conflict or problem into a set of questions and answers, Baudrillard (1983:121) argues. And reality, tested in this way, is decoded according to the same pattern: it is decoded according to the same code, inscribed in each message and motif as miniaturised genetic code. Everything is presented today in a spreadsheet series or as part of a series of products and this fact itself is already testing you, since you have to make decisions. This approximates your general attitude to the outside world with a reading and a selective decipherment. We live less as users than readers and voters, who read cells in a spread-sheet. But still: for the same reason that you are constantly selected and tested by the medium itself.

Gilles Deleuze (2003:11) reproduces what painter Francis Bacon says when talking about photography: it is not a form of what one sees, it is what the modern man sees. This is problematic not only because the photographic image is figurative, but since the photograph is alleged to control the seeing and thus rules over the painting. Does this mean that the contemporary man sees something that the historic man could not see? Is it something learned or acquired? Can we break away from the conventions we were brought up within? Is a photo of a road that disappears into the horizon something more than what we can sense with our eyes and the interpretations our brain makes of what we see? What does Deleuze mean by controlling our vision as modern people? What once started as a camera obscura – a help to draw from the outside world – may be drawings of images existing in our brains in the form of photographs. Does that mean that all the photographs we have seen, or at least those that have made an impression on us, whether we are aware of it or not, are embedded in our memory? If so, they should affect us forever.

Photography is an evolutionary phenomenon, writes Ali Hossaini (2003:1), not a fixed process and it has drastically changed society at every stage of refinement. From simple devices, the medium has been branched out into a huge family of technologies that include film, television and digital images. Individuals use cameras, but the media technology is far more powerful in the hands of companies and the state. Optical media entertain and inform, impress and repress, they permeate everyday life. What links snapshots and surveillance footage together? Cultural theorists see the social effects of mass media, ranging from liberation to extreme dehumanisation, but the origin of these effects has not been described. The origin of the content in the media lives in that way in a state of limbo, notes Hossaini. Does it mean that the content of all the media clinging to us to talk about something new about ourselves that we had no idea about?

What remains then? Is a photograph the remnant that remains when man disappears from life? Albert Camus (1955:51) pondered this. For some reason, the actor has chosen fame, a fame that is sanctified and tested. From the fact that everything will die one day, he draws the best conclusion. An actor does succeed or does not succeed. A writer has some hope, though he is not appreciated. He assumes that his work will testify to what he was. At best, the actor leaves us with a photograph of himself and nothing of what he himself was, his gestures and his silence, his gasping or his loving gasp, will be brought down to us. For the actor, not being known to not act and not acting is to die a hundred times with all the creatures that he could have brought to life or revived, Camus says. Anyone who fails to become famous may still be living in saved photo albums in the attic of some grandchild.

The remarkable thing about photography is that although photography has a story, or several stories, there is no history for individual photographs in the same way as it is for literary texts or paintings, claims British linguist Clive Scott (2007: 124). Scott believes that there is also no overall knowledge of photographs and the emerging interpretation of photographic images. This means that every time we encounter a photographic image, we have to start all over. It is about, Scott believes, that we must free ourselves from the relatively unmediated perceptual encounter, from the awareness of our ignorance so that we create our own way of absorbing the image and allowing it to create meaning in our lives. Other writers claim that since its invention, photography has explored various symbiotic relationships with language, that language is not only a constant companion to photographic images, but implicated in the very process of viewing photographs. We often use the language to describe images.

Maybe there are some iconic photographs that have become as well-known as novels, such as the "Peace Kiss" in Paris?

According to this way of regarding photography, it does not exist on its own. Instead, the existence of photography is intimately linked to how we view photographs with the help of language. Maybe photography has an existence outside of language – and expresses its meaning in a different way than what we traditionally call language? We return to this idea, there are thinkers who believe that photography does not work without accompanying text.

We speak about imagery and design language in terms of photographs, in a way similar to what we use when we speak or write about painted images, music or fiction.

It is perfectly in order to use the vocabulary, should we

invent a new one for each object we consider there is the risk that we would soon get lost in the language.

The French film theorist André Bazin (1967:13) compares photography to painting and argues that, the originality of photography lies mainly in its objective nature. Bazin makes the point that camera lenses are called precisely lenses, in French "objectif". Hence the role of the photographic image being 'objective'. For the first time, an image of the world is formed automatically, without any creative intervention by man. The photographer's personality enters the process only through his choice of subject to be photographed and through the purpose the photographer has in mind. Although the end result may reflect some of the photographer's personality, this does not mean that it plays the same role as the painter's personality. All artistic expressions are based on human presence, only photography creates an advantage of human absence. Photo affects us as phenomenon in nature, like a flower or a snowflake whose origin is an inseparable part of their beauty. Bazin also spins thoughts about the fact that photographic images work as co-players or opponents in our lives. Are we so intimately connected with the images we consider to be about interaction that we constantly interact with them? What do photographers say about being compared to machine operators?

As Solveig Jülich (2006:230) notes in connection with the 1897 Art and Industrial Exhibition in Stockholm, media throughout history have been continuously associated and interacting with each other. It can range from a simple comparison or exchange of some kind to a more radical change in the media involved. The term intermediality refers to how different audience positions have been compared and paired with each other in specific historical situations. The development is thus difficult to figure out, but we can safely assume that photography and drawing / painting have cross-fertilised each other as forms of expression.

French film theorist André Bazin (1967:14) discusses man's approach to photography. As far as photography is concerned, it is a very realistic image of reality and we tend to treat photography as an object in itself. Only a photographic lens can give us the kind of image of the object that is capable of meeting the deep need that humans have of replacing it with something more than just an approximation, a kind of decal or transmission, Bazin says. The photographic image is the object itself, the object is freed from the conditions of the time and space in which it was made. No matter how blurred, distorted or discolored, regardless of whether the image may be in the absence of documentary value, it shares through the very process of its creation, the existence of the model it is a reproduction of, it is the model. Hence the charm of family albums. These grey or sepia-tinted shadows, phantom-like and almost indistinct images, no longer traditional family portraits but rather the disturbing presence of life halted at a definite moment in its existence, freed from its fate – though not as prestige art but by virtue of a mechanical process. Photography does not create eternity, as art does, it embalms time, it simply saves it from its own past. It seems Bazin thinks that photography is, in its essence, more documentation than anything else.

Pierre Bourdieu (1990:5) uses the German philosopher

Friedrich Hegel to describe the bad treatment that early photography was given: You could say about photography what Hegel said about philosophy: *"No other art or science is subjected to this last degree of contempt , assuming that we are the master of it right away."* Unlike more "culturally demanding activities" such as drawing, painting or playing a musical instrument, as opposed to visiting museums or concerts, photography does not require either academically schooled culture or apprenticeship and the "profession" that devotes its value to cultural consumption and practice, usually considered to be the most noble, by withholding it from the man in the street. Bourdieu describes how photography has also become the domain of the "lower" classes because the cultural elite does not regard photography as art. This may have meant that the development of photography could have proceeded without constant attention from the cultural elite and thus been able to flower on its own. The photograph has been regarded as a craft without the opportunity to shoulder the status of the artwork.

Even when the production of the image is completely handed over to the camera's automatic exposure, the exposure of the image is still a choice that involves aesthetic and ethical values, Bourdieu (1990:6) argues. If, in the abstract, nature and development of photographic technology tends to make everything objectively "photographic", it is still true that among the theoretically infinite number of photographs that are technically possible, each group chooses a finite and well-defined spectrum of subjects, genres and compositions. In Friedrich Nietzsche's words: *"The artist chooses his motives. That's his way of praising.*" Since it is a "choice that praises", because it seeks to capture, that is, to solemnise and perpetuate, photography cannot be left to the randomness in the individual's imagination and through the mediation of ethos, the internalisation of objective and common regularities. The group places this practice under its collective rule so that the most trivial photographs express, apart from the photographer's explicit intentions, an entire group's common system of systems of perception, thinking and appreciation. The group is responsible for the overall valuation of the photograph, Bourdieu says. Although in some contexts we encounter thoughts like that a work of art is always a work of art, even though no man has had the opportunity to consider the supposed work of art.

French photographer Henri Cartier-Bresson describes his view of what photography is in this way:

"For me, photography is a simultaneous recognition, at a fraction of a second, of the importance of an event, as well as an exact organisation of the forms that give the event its proper expression. I believe that it is through the act of life that the discovery of our own self is continually made with the discovery of the world around us that can shape us, but which can also be influenced by us. A balance must be established between these two worlds – one within us and one outside us. As a result of a constant reciprocal process, these worlds will form a single. And it is this world that we must communicate. " (my translation) (1952:18)

Cartier-Bresson also seems to think that the role of photography is to bridge the distance between the world and the individual, or between society and the individual. Since Cartier-Bresson was photographing on the street, without directing his motives, he is interested in the rapid process of street photography.

American photographer W. Eugene Smith, with a long career as a war photographer and as a collaborator in Life and other large post-war magazines, wrote about the photograph as "the little voice":

"Photography is primarily a small voice, which sometimes, not always, with a picture or a collection convinces our minds in a way that leads to awareness. It depends entirely on the viewer; some photographs evoke such feelings that they generate reflection. This can lead an individual or, who knows, many of us, to listen to reason." (1983)

Thus, although the photograph is a small voice, it can, according to Smith, at good moments affect the viewer. Maybe this is what we are looking for in photographs, influence, or something that grabs us anyway. Something we believe contains significance. that creates a meaning for us, or a kind of story.

Pierre Bourdieu (1990:76) argues that the whole paradox of popular photography is revealed by its time dimension. An instant cut into the visible world gives photography the tools to dissolve the fixed and compact reality of everyday perception of an infinity of volatile profiles as dream images to capture absolutely unique moments of mutual situations of things, to understand, as Walter Benjamin has shown, aspects, imperceptible because they are instantaneous, of the perceived world, to stop human gestures in the absurdity of a now consisting of "salt pillars". Is it about capturing the volatile, shaping it and thus building monuments from it? Is it about a world that Benjamin and Bourdieu regard as a floating kaleidoscope of moments we will never be able to really see?

Victor Burgin (1980:51) points out that although photography is a "visual medium", it is not a wholly visual medium. He does not merely point to the fact that we rarely see a photographic image in use that is not accompanied by writing (although this is a very significant fact). Even the headless "art photography", framed and isolated on the gallery wall, is invaded by the language at the moment it is viewed: in memory, through associations, fragments of words and images are mixed and exchanged. It will be objected that this is an unclear and insignificant background noise for our primary act of seeing. The garbage from our blood circulation is even more unclear, says Burgin, but no less important for it.

Meeting the past

Lisa Gitelman (2006:5) considers photography as a meeting with the past. A photographic image offers a two-dimensional, visual representation of its subject, but it is also unique as evidence, an index, since the photograph was created in the moment of the past it represents. Other encounters with the past may be less clear, less causal and less indexical, such as when viewers with a TV news broadcast are transported "live" to the outside of a building where something happened a little while ago, or when digital images further complicate the notion of a photographic image altogether. We make some kind of journey in time permeated by time zones, here it is about what has been, what is now and possibly what is to come. We have the opportunity to handle the past, present and the future in the same arena, that is, in photography.

Joanna Sassoon (2007:301ff) is regarding photography as the product of the confluence of technology, the photographer's eye and the developer's hand; processes described as containing "aura of alchemy" given the combination of specific knowledge required to produce fine photographic objects – whether simple daguerreotypes or fine enlargements. Its materiality has been an integral part of a photographic object since in the earliest photographic processes when they were only produced as a single concrete object. Embedded in the photographic object, clues are visible to a trained eye that reveals the subtle relationships between negatives, papers, and the processes used to physically produce the image. The dimensions of photographic objects are an indicator of the camera, negative format, date of manufacture. Textures and tonal intervals are clues to the photographic processes when used to produce the images. Information including notes on the back of the photographs also provides additional information such as captions, retouching details and instructions for cropping. As Geoffrey Batchen writes, photography is an image that can have "volume, opacity, tactility and physical presence in the world" (Batchen, 1997:2) – essentially an aura of materiality that originates from the original photographic object. While present in original photographic objects and vintage prints, the quality that arises from its original material form is difficult to imitate and is often completely lost in photographic copies with modern materials. The fact that the photographic paper copy is an object with its own identity is the central point in Sassoon's reasoning, but her description also indicates that the analog photographic technique had properties that are missing from the inkjet printed digital photographic image.

The term "original", says Sassoon (2007:302), works differently for photography than for other forms of documents or works of art. In technical and photographic terms, the negative is the original because it is the medium that records what is in front of the lens at the time of exposure. But as John Berger (1980:291) writes: "*the very principle of photography is that the resulting image is not unique, but on the contrary infinitely reproducible*". While the negative may in fact be "the most true documentation" of what was in front of the lens, it is when you perceive this negative as the only original in the photographic process that you *"emphasise the unique in front of the purpose"*. You can argue that while the negative can be seen as the original in photographic terms, the document that conveys the message is the copy from the negative. So, the analog technique allows photography to take a complicated path until it finally lies in front of the viewer's eyes.

During its lifespan, the photographic image may potentially move between multiple locations and at each change of ownership and context new meanings are acquired. The photograph gets its meaning and evidential power from the contexts in which it is placed and when the contexts are removed it becomes an isolated and partially meaningless object, says Sassoon (2007: 304).

Provenance is important for viewing the image, the way the image is made to fall under the viewer's scrutiny is of importance.

Jean Baudrillard (2002:117) argues that photography, together with film and painting, is based on the fact that there is a scene and a viewer – and through this different from video art and art on a computer screen. In the latter cases, viewing is more about immersion – a sinking, a kind of umbilical cord, a kind of "tactile" interaction that Marshall McLuhan once noted about television. A cellular, corpuscular immersion: you enter the fluid substance of the image, possibly to change it, in the same way that science infiltrates the genetic code to transform the body itself. You move as you please, you do what you want from the interactive image, but immersion is the price of this endless availability, this open combination of elements. It is the same with the "virtual" text, any virtual text (Internet, word processing).

This worked as in a computer-generated image – something that no longer bears any relation to the gaze's exceeding or writing. As soon as you are in front of the screen, Baudrillard (2002:178) notes, you can no longer see the text as text, but as an image.

Now, in the strict distinction between text and screen, between text and image, writing is an activity in itself, never an interaction. Similarly, it is only with a strict distinction between stage and salon that the spectator is a participant in his own right.

Everything today is conspiring to abolish this separation: the spectator is brought into a user-friendly, interactive immersion. The highlight of the spectator or his / her ending? When everyone is an actor, there is no action anymore, no scene. End of the aesthetic illusion.

Machines only produce machines. This is becoming increasingly true as the virtual technologies evolve. At a certain level of intrigue, of immersion in virtual machines, there is no longer any distinction between man and machine: the machine stands on both sides of the interface. Maybe you are just the space of the machine now – man has become the virtual reality of the machine, its mirror operator. This has to do with the very nature of the monitor, writes Baudrillard (2002:178). There is no "through" screen in the way there is a "through" the mirror. The measures of time itself merge there in "real time". The hallmark of all virtual space is first and foremost to be there, to be empty and thus capable of being filled with something. It is up to you to enter in real time for interactivity with the void.

Similarly, everything produced with the help of machines is a machine, Baudrillard (2002:178) states. The texts, pictures, films, speech and programs that come from computers are machine products and they carry the functions of these products, they are constructed in an artificial way, face lift of the machine; the movies are filled with special effects, the lyrics full of repetitions due to the machine's malicious willingness to function at all costs (which is its passion) and the operator's fascination with its boundless possibilities to function. Technology leads us to hibernation, or we may risk creating something that does not suit us.

Hence the tired characters in movies with all this violence and the pornographic sexuality, which are merely special effects of violence and sex, no longer even fantasised by humans, but purely mechanical violence that no longer affects us. This explains, Baudrillard (2002:178) states, all these texts that are similar to the work of "intelligent" virtual agents, whose only act is programming, the rest is played out along purely automatic lines. This has nothing to do with automatic writing (*ecriture automatique*) that hinted at the magical zooming of words and concepts, while all we have here is a programmed automatically, an automatic review of all possibilities. Scroll with the machine's design of the body, the text, the image. This is called cybernetics: controlling the image, the text, the body from the inside, so to speak from its pattern, by playing with its code or the genetic information. It is this anguish of the ideal performance of text or image, the possibility of endlessly correcting, that produces in the "creative artist" this dizziness of interactivity with his own motive, alongside the troubled dizziness over not having reached the technical limitations. We have, Baudrillard seems to mean, ourselves, with the machines creating a cybernetic photographic image.

Jean Baudrillard (2009:21) poses the question of why not everything has already disappeared and discusses what visual art is all about, perhaps to nurture the traces of objects that we would otherwise consider to have disappeared. On the contrary, vanishing can be a desire to see what the world looks like in our absence (photography) or to look beyond the end, beyond the subject, beyond all meaning, beyond the horizon of vanishing, if there is still a world, an unprogrammed version of the thing. An area of pure appearance, of the world as it is (and not of the real world, which is always just a world of representation), which can arise only from the disappearance of all added value.

Jean Baudrillard notes that the art, which does not know that it has disappeared, continues to take place, in a vegetative state:

The art itself in modern times exists only on the basis of its disappearance – not only the art of doing the real art disappears and displaces it with another scene, but the art of abolishing itself during its practice (Hegel). It was by doing this that it constituted an event, that it was crucial. I say "was" on purpose, for art today, even though it has disappeared, does not know that it has disappeared and – this is the worst – continues on its path in a vegetative state. (2009:22)

So the art is included in the game, but according to Baudrillard it does not add much. It has landed in a state that is passive – possibly because it has exhausted its possibilities. Or, because the viewer does not make demands on what is art.

Gilles Deleuze (2003: 8) argues that painting must extract the figure from the figurative. However, according to Deleuze, Francis Bacon cites two developments which seem to indicate that modern painting has a different relation to figuration or illustration than the painting had in the past. Firstly, photography has taken over the illustrative and documentary role, so that modern painting no longer has to fulfill this function, which still burdens previous painters. Secondly, painting used to depend on certain "religious possibilities" which still gave an illustrated meaning to figuration, while modern painting is an atheistic game. Does this mean that the "religious possibilities" return with the photograph?

Jonathan Crary (1990:13) argues that photographs may have some obvious similarities to older types of images, such as perspective painting or drawings made using a camera obscura, but in the system burst in which photography is a carrier of such similarities that are insignificant. Photography may be argued to being a part of a new and homogeneous area of consumption and circulation where a viewer gets stuck. To understand the "photographic effect" of the nineteenth century, one must see it as an important component of a new cultural economy of value and exchange, not as a carrier with a continuous history of visual representation.

Although it is instant, photography has a completely different ambition than representing, illustrating, or telling Gilles Delueze (2003:8-9) notes, pointing to the advantages of fast technology. It is about a seemingly fast technology for image production that gives room for questions and ambitions.

It is too easy to show that this social representation is based on false evidence and prejudice, Bourdieu (1990: 73-74) argued, in fact photography captures an aspect of reality that is always only the result of an arbitrary choice and consequently of a transcription. One of all qualities of the object are the only ones that remain, the visual qualities that appear for a moment and from a single point of view. These are transcribed in black and white, generally on a reduced scale and always projected in one plane. In other words, photography is a conventional system that expresses space in terms of perspective laws and volumes and colors in terms of variations between black and white. Photography is generally considered to be a perfectly realistic and objective record of the visible world as it (since its birth) has been assigned social uses that are considered "realistic" and "objective". If it has immediately presented itself with all the precedents of a symbolic communication without syntax, in short a "natural language", this is especially so since the selection it makes from the visible world is logically completely in line with the representation of the world that has dominated Europe since the 15th century. Does this reasoning mean that digital technology represents a historical break with this representation?

Both popular and theoretical discourses on photography have, since the beginning of photography, been permeated with ideas of spirituality, mysticism and the supernatural, says Tomanić Trivundža (2014: 218). Photographic images have been granted certain powers in addition to their mere ability to depict an object or scene: they have come to be seen as seductive, dangerous, suggestive or enlightening, insinuating the presence or origin of mythical, magical or divine powers.

Does photography create "false memories", some kind of direction that really has nothing to do with the original subject? When we made the picture, we "saved" the bit of time we had just experienced. But is photography so much more informative than our own memory? I can admit that a picture from the past toggles my brain. We can even "remember" parts of the picture that are not even visible in the photograph. "There was a kiosk behind that house."

It is probably true that there was a kiosk behind the house at the time of the photo shoot. Since we can't see it in the photo, it's not in the photo, right? Is it the information about the place we stored and not something that the photograph contains? The photograph is without doubt what triggers the memory of the "kiosk".

Does this mean that photography has agency, that is, can affect the viewer? Or is it a direction that arises in the viewer's brain? Anyone who has not been to the site has no memory of the hidden kiosk and it would be too much to assume that the "meaning" of the photograph would be transmitted to such a viewer as well. The information about the kiosk is thus reserved for the viewer who has knowledge of the geographical location at a given time when there was a kiosk behind the house.

Political actors and professionals in the media often talk about the (superior) power of images to influence individual perceptions and to mobilise or swing group thinking, a process that under normal circumstances is considered overwhelmed by emotion, of some "added value" to the images themselves, says Tomanić Trivundža (2014:218). Theoretical writings on photography often mark "deficiency" in the language to explain the visual, or give up their pursuit of meaning, the most well-known case of the latter concerns Roland Barthes (2014:178), whose analytical semiotic apparatus capitulated in front of a family photograph in *Camera Lucida*. Or, rather, as I always regarded it, to have been a weakness in *Camera Lucida*, the photograph that is the foundation of the main thinking is not found within the book.

The importance of perspective attaches importance

argues André Bazin (1967:11) and notes that the decisive moment undoubtedly came with the discovery of the first scientific and already in some sense mechanical system of reproduction, namely the perspective: Leonardo Da Vinci's camera obscura in the forbidden camera in Niepce. The artist was now in a position to create the illusion of a three-dimensional space in which objects appeared to exist as our eyes in reality see them. From there on, art painting is torn between two ambitions: one primarily aesthetic, that is the expression of the spiritual reality in which the symbol transcends its model and the other purely psychological, that is, the doubling of the world outside. The fulfillment of this appetite for illusion only serves to increase it, bit by bit, to consume visual art. Since perspectives had only solved the problem of form and not movement, realism had to continue the search for some way to dramatically express the moment of a kind of psychic fourth dimension that could suggest life in the tortured immobility of the Baroque art.

Photographs are not merely a mechanical depiction, says John Berger (1972:10), each image embodies a way of seeing, even a photographic image. Every time we look at a photo, we are aware, albeit to a lesser degree, that the photographer has chosen that particular image from an infinity of other possible subjects. This also applies to the most relaxed family pictures. The photographer's way of seeing is reflected in his subject choices. The painter's way of seeing is reconstituted by the marks he makes on the canvas or paper.

Although each image embodies a way of seeing, our perception or assessment of an image also depends on our own way of seeing. I may see something in a photograph that you don't see and vice versa. Who should decide who doesn't see the "right thing"?

Of course, photography as an art form has its followers. André Bazin (1960:8) believes that photography can surpass traditional art in creative power. The painter's aesthetic world is of a different kind than the world around him. Its boundaries encompass a significantly and substantially different microcosm. Photography as such and the object itself have a common existence, like the connection between a finger a its fingerprint. Therefore, photography actually contributes something to the natural creation rather than offering a replacement for it. So here is the connection that many people find themselves between the photographed and the final photographic image.

Latour & Hermant (1998: 41) describe a situation at Café de Flore in Paris where a couple of North American tourists are staring at another couple sitting in the room. The first couple has made a photograph of the second, a TYPICAL photograph – a *cliché*. Is there a more Parisian scene than lovers engaged in passionate conversation, unaware of their surroundings, the glasses and waiters, the academic who reads his newspaper, the cafe owner and his business affairs; indifferent even to tourists, which so typically, snaps pictures of them. "*Just like a Doisneau,*" one American says to the other, "*Paris is always Paris*", "*Plus ça change, plus c'est pareil*". ("The more it changes, the more it stays the same"). We all have expectations of life and have our heads full of stereotypical thoughts on how things ought to be. The risk may be that we are only looking for scenes and motifs that confirm our notions of what, for example Paris, should give us in the form of photographic images. The risk of ending with a cliché is imminent. It may not be bad either, it is clichés and stereotypes that help to make the world understandable.

Iconoclash – criticism and praise come together

At a comprehensive art exhibition in 2002, Bruno Latour used the term "iconoclash" to define the dynamics of the fascinating, seemingly universal cultural phenomenon: our love-hate relationship with images. Peter Gibian (2011) describes how Bruno Latour introduced the concept of "iconoclash". The term was, in Latour's opinion, necessary to convey the dual nature of the process by which iconoclasm – man's desire to criticise and destroy images so often expressed in conjunction with his twin and apparent opposite of iconophilia or idolatry, the human impulse to be enchanted by visual figures. For Latour, this dialectical shift between the iconoclasm and the iconophilia is experienced by the human subject as the two incompatible impulses always seem to occur together, prompting us at the same moment, even when they force us in opposite directions.

From a sociological perspective, photography and film, according to André Bazin (1967:10), could give a natural explanation to the great spiritual and technological crisis that befell modern painting around the mid-19th century. According to Bazin, Andre Malraux has described the film as the ultimate development to date of malleable realism, starting in the Renaissance and with its most complete expression in Baroque art. Has the century-old conflict in the view of the difference between painting and photography been merely evil? Or has it driven the development of both art forms further?

The viewer's influence on the emotions of photography

The story that possibly lives within a photographic image is transformed into new stories when new viewers are confronted with the image. New stories emerge for each new viewer who meets the photograph. Of course, this is because it is within the viewer that, among other things, the traces and experiences of the viewer's past extracts stories from the image. It is not only because the image itself has a billion stories to present to new viewers.

In the stories that are retrieved, some viewers have their own favourite. It turns out when two viewers discuss a photograph they both saw and think is "good". Here, possibly two or more very different stories will emerge and the stories may be overlapping or as far apart as is imaginable. We definitely think that it doesn't appear to be the same photograph they have seen. However, it points to the idea that Mitchell (2005) has raised. Does the image live with any kind of direction built into its content? As if the picture had its own will with the different stories. It seems undeniably to be that way and it seems that there is no image strong enough to stop this "force" or "expression" emanating from the photographs. Maybe we will never really "understand" photographs in the same way as other viewers. As I see it, it is an exciting, but terribly diverse, flora of stories generated by the images we create.

The varied range of stories that arise in a way when the

viewer "reflects" in a photographic image means that there is no upper limit to how many stories that may actually emanate from a single photograph. If we multiply that number by the number of possible viewers, we experience staggering amounts of possible stories that theoretically have the potential to grow as more viewers are exposed to a photograph. We may assume that the viewers are somewhat reminiscent of each other, but that is not something they really need to be. They can all come as a force of "new" viewers. We must keep in mind that it is these viewers' own memories, experiences or knowledge that are reflected in the photograph. They create one or more stories in the mind of the viewer. It is about what we usually classify as "emotions", an experience that has dug deep into the mind's base of ideas about the world: without them we would not be able to communicate in any way, not even with traditional linguistics. Does that mean that communication is about imagery? We must probably describe the relationship between viewer and image as a communication exchange. This, which is probably basically about linguistic meetings – between people – can dig more or less profound. We never know which demons we stir up from within when we study a new photograph. It is undoubtedly an exciting journey to embark on – looking at photographic images. Were it not for us as viewers to be curious, we would never experience any images that grab hold of us. As if it were possible to avoid, since our gaze constantly reads the surroundings and constant deviations from what we have learned is the benchmark of normality. Without that view, consideration or no consideration, no images would be made as there would be no "market" for them. We simply wouldn't see any point in producing images sent out in a black hole of disinterest. Instead, we grow up and learn that everyone, really everyone, is interested in watching. There are no exceptions, although some claim this.

We are constantly seeking new experiences for our eyes. We collect information that triggers an emotional reaction in our interior. In short, it is about getting a kind of endorphin rush from seeing our outside world in new constellations, in parts, severely cropped or in combinations we have not previously encountered.

Is there any reason to assume that images and, above all, photographs are loaded with the emotions of their subjects and that these can come across to the viewer in the form of emotions? C. J. Ducasse (1964) made an attempt to sort this out in the 1960s, then phenomenologists had in their own way been studying the subject. Above all existential phenomenologists such as Hannah Arendt, Simone de Beauvoir, Martin Heidegger, Emmanuel Levinas, Jean-Paul Sartre and Maurice Merleau-Ponty. In these texts I have mainly leaned towards the latter two.

We may ask ourselves if the emotions we feel, in the form of feelings, are present in a photograph in the world we can see, or if it is an interaction with our experiences, so that we project emotions into a photograph and then experience those who like photography make us react in this way? Have these emotions been created by a kind of cross fertilisation of the characters found in photography and our learned way of interpreting them?

Is the message of a photography a reflection of what our psyche wants the photograph to contain? Those who begin to study photographs often find it daunting that the need to see more and more photographs gradually becomes stronger. The image browsing tends to develop into a kind of image archery. Viewing photographs generates experiences and experiences generate the need to see more photographs.

What is the viewer seeing? Without knowledge and own experience, the viewer sees nothing more than some sort of shadow on a flat surface. In order for us to recognise a forest, we must have learned to understand the concept – in order to see something as an expression of anxiety we must have a prior knowledge of the concept of anxiety. We can't really find something we aren't already familiar with. Then the mix in the artwork can be such that new relationships between the parts known to the viewer are created. The images we consider consist of a selection of images based on an almost infinite amount. Some of all these images catch our attention and cause us to more or less sink into the images.

Some of the images capture us in a more profound way than others and we share our inner by allowing this to be reflected and the image can re-enter our psyche. Of all the possible images we can consider, only those we get stuck with, or in, mean a lot to us. In this way, in the role of viewer, we are on our way to get into the picture, at the same time as it enters us.

We live for a short time in a kind of symbiosis with the image, during the time we consider it. In this exchange, the "experience" takes place that we can download from the image, the impact on us that images radiate. Here, the transfer of emotions, from the viewer, to the image, results in our perceived emotions.

During this exchange of emotions, the viewer feels that the image has a “meaning”, that is, means something that is unique to this viewer and will not be repeated when the next viewer sees the image. Possibly not even when the same viewer sees the image again. Or the exact same series of emotional activation will take place when the next viewer steps onto the stage and this happens even though it may be since this new viewer has similar luggage to the first. It is this that Pierre Bourdieu (1990) describes as “habitus”, which gives the kinship between the two consecutive viewers. They can be said to carry the same kind of fine cultural luggage. Habitus can be regarded as embodied capital. A human habitus is thus a product of her life history. I think this describes the “backpack” of experiences we carry with us through life. In this text I do not go deeper into this.

Perhaps this is why the “cultural elite” views art in its own special way and in some cases photography considers it an attack on (painting) art. It can be said that you who “understand” art in the “established” way have a suitable background for this by carrying a cultural capital that is a prerequisite for this interpretation of art.

Those who do not carry the right cultural capital will not experience the art in the manner defined by the cultural establishment. Implicit: the right way. Therefore, it is a wrong way for the holder of the right cultural capital. We must therefore pay attention to the difference marked by the cultural elite. The elite has also for a long time looked at photography as an art expression, perhaps for the only reason that it does not always take a month from the idea until the photograph hangs on the wall – a production time that may apply for example to art painting. Although the photographic image is not a work of the moment, as it has occasionally been claimed. It takes time and the practitioner probably gets better at his work over time.

The contemplation, on the other hand, can be a work of the moment. Either the image captures the viewer or the viewer captures the image. That attraction can be immediate. There may be pictures that "grow" at a second or third view. This is probably because the viewer's mood is different during the third viewing. The viewer is more focused on consuming the current image.

The emotion we experience viewing these images is something that is triggered from the outside, but that is experienced inside. They are thus already in place in us viewers when we enter a gallery and for the first time look at the pictures. It is a reaction that occurs at the point where we observe this image for the first time. Then our past image we study links to the present as if it is an experience we have now – even though it is triggered by something that happened then, that is in the past tense.

The experiences

The hope of radically changing life is no longer in the brain, but has ended up in the heart, writes French philosopher Michel Lacroix (2001) in the essay collection "Le culte de l'émotion". The book is about the hunt for experiences, or kicks. Every epoch in history has its human ideal, from the Renaissance to today's individualistic human ideal, which Lacroix thinks is *Homo sentient – the emotional human.* The logical parts of the brain are left behind when you push behind the soul's traditional shell and focus on the "primitive" feelings. Lacroix tries to describe the mechanisms behind the emotional experiences of the addict, which drives us to chase "kicks". Through bungy jumping or other extreme activities we show other people where we belong. The emotional cult and body culture are interdependent. Emotions have the advantage that they also affect the body.

The advertising message reflects the social soul, Lacroix says, and it is because advertising portray the social soul since advertising can show the Grand Canyon from a helicopter, snowboarders in the Chilean winter snow, Brazilian rhythms and elephant rides in Sri Lanka. These advertising themes are about emotions, feeling that you are experiencing something, preferably adventurous. Adventures is what modern man lacks. Since the outside world does not give me value for my actions, it remains only for me to use the power I have over my own soul. How does this focus on the emotions come about? Lacroix thinks it is a kind of compensation mechanism. The emotional storms replace the emptiness we experience because of the loss of hope for the future. That hope has disappeared for us through the changes of society. We are, according to Lacroix, created for a different life than many in the Western world today live.

We are made to cope with physical challenges, but these kinds of challenges are few in modern society.

Instead, we are subjected to overstimulation of the senses, we can experience the speed through the camera on the Formula 1 race car and watch images that were previously reserved for the people who drove the car. We can take advantage of what Lacroix calls “the shamanic trance” by, for example, dancing at a rave party. The geography of the world has been given a different role in that we can traverse the Amazon rainforests on the “right” journeys where we only experience the best pieces of the cake. What Lacroix calls the “perverse challenge” balances almost on the criminal scale, like becoming a serial killer or the like. Most of us are content to watch movies and read books about similar things in our spare time.

This results in our emotional life being depleted and we need real kicks to feel good. Lacroix sees two types of experiences / feelings; partly the contemplative, which lasts for a long time, and the one that more shakes up our nervous system with impressions and emotions, but passes rather quickly. Those who become accustomed to the latter type hunt like a junkie for constantly new kicks, while those who settle for the quieter variant need not hunt in the same way.

As the philosopher he is, Michel Lacroix believes that the more contemplative experience / emotions rewards the individual the most in the long run. The second type of kick is fast-paced and resembles too much a junkie's fix to be really healthy.

The Zeitgeist

Are we about to become copies of the people we see on TV? Is the world on its way to develop into a gigantic karaoke show, as the founder of the punk group Sex Pistols, Malcolm McLaren, claimed? Why do many of us think it is in order to broadcast television programs like “Aim for the Stars” where people copy what others have done? What influences us to change our clothes, our ideas and our expressions to newer variants? Is there a "skill" in imitating others, being each other's replicants? Is there any similarity magic in this, that if I use the same branded products as the people I want to be like, I'm becoming closer to them?

Some of these questions music journalist Patrice Bollon (2002) tries out in the book "*Esprit d'Époque*". It is no small task. Bollon works methodically, with sweeping generalisations that provide some interesting angles on what and which affect us. What, then, is the least common denominator in what we call the "spirit of the times"? We have the ability to see a car, a piece of clothing, a piece of furniture or hear a song and place it quite well in time. Of course, this is because there is a kinship between most of what is produced and consumed during a particular era.

When it comes to clothing, they are also affected by "fashion", although not as radical as with haute couture. This means that we who are referred to shop at H&M, IKEA or Intersport will remind each other. We go around as ticking proof that time is "now" and a decade later it is just as clearly "then". The things we buy must remind us of something, maybe we have seen some prominent person wearing something similar. One of the most well-known products in the western world is "Chanel no 5" which was introduced in 1921. Marilyn Monroe gave the perfume extra help when in an interview in the 1950s on the question of how she was dressed when she slept answered: - *In Chanel no 5 !*

Neither Yves Saint Laurent's "Opium" launched in 1977 nor Calvin Klein's "CK One" from 1996 have yet reached the five-year success, although "CK One" took a good part of the market. Chanel no 5 has had many more years. Perhaps our need for role models is so deeply rooted that it is impossible to live without being influenced by others, even if we guard ourselves against everything we can? But, that is exactly what we are not doing, right what it is, we have changed and do not really know how it went.

Who copies who? Do I think that three days of beard stubble and clean-shaven skull are in order because I have seen a broken Bruce Willis with those attributes in enough films? Do I want to be Bruce Willis? Or is it about wanting to get close to Zen Buddhist monks, skinheads, rappers, Kojak or Yul Brynner? By shaving my head, I show a kind of value community with others in the same situation. But it can go wrong.

Wide shoulders are something our clothes can help us get if we can't put in the time it takes to trim the body. Or if nature has been nice to us by making us narrow-hipped. The fashion creators generate by accentuating the shoulders of the female fashion a more feminine look, even though broad shoulders are a traditional masculine desire, Bollon argues.

During the period from the turn of the century to the outbreak of the First World War in 1914, the hairdressers of the European continent provided for curly hair. The fashion slaves could look like they had a sheepskin on their heads. It had its origins in the fact that there were notions that curly hair made a more lovely impression, while straight hair on the other hand represented the "wild". At about the same time, there was still the 18th-century remnant that a pale face signalled aristocracy. Sun tan showed that you had to stay outdoors, probably to make your living. Interesting is how this class mark completely changed meaning. Today, at our latitudes, it is a sign of prosperity with half-deep tan, while it is considered a bit "trashy" to sunbathe towards mahogany tones. Not to mention all the notions of cancer that a deep tone of the skin gives.

In the 1920s, portrait photographers took "natural" photographs, with the light equally bright on both sides of the model. In the 1930s it became fashion with stronger light from one side. This meant that the other half of the face became darker. During the 50's, soft images became fashion. During the 1960s, the photo portrait became more iconic with the object in the middle.

We get through conversations with insights into how others think. Others adjust to our thinking and we get a kind of karaoke effect. We try, but we cannot escape our fate as "replicants". We may not be able to avoid becoming replicants if we live with others and influence them while affecting us? In many ways, that seems to be what society is all about.

It is possible that the "time's spirit" with the constant search for adrenaline kicks is a hunt for emotions, which in turn gives the body answers in the form of feelings about what we do.

How are emotions created in photography?

C. J. Ducasse (1964) has made an attempt to sort this out regarding emotions in photographs. Ducasse believes that the transmission of the expressed emotions occurs or is not largely unintentional since a work of art may never be noticed by anyone other than the artist himself and yet remains a work of art. The first fact worth noting is that the word art in its basic meaning means skill and that the purposes of the pursuit of skill may be more specifically pragmatic, epistemic, or aesthetic. Exactly where does the creative activity that can be called expression of emotions consist of what the artist does at the time he creates a work of art? What does it mean to say that the artwork, when it exists, itself "expresses emotions"? A more just account of what is really claimed when art is said to be the language of emotions would be that art is the language of emotion.

John Dewey (1980:35) published his book "Art as experience" in the 1930s when modern times broke into the western world and Dewey pondered the relationship between art and the experience of art. Dewey said that things are experienced, but not in such a way that they are composed for an experience. There is distraction and dissemination; what we observe and what we think, what we want and what we get are at odds with each other. We put our hands on the plow and return; we start and then we end because of irreversible interruptions or internal lethargy. Contrary to such experience, Dewey said, we have an experience when the perceived material follows its course to fulfillment. Then and only then is it integrated into and delimited by the general stream of experiences from other experiences.

A job is completed satisfactorily; a problem gets its solution; a game is played through; a situation, whether it be eating a meal, playing a game of chess, having a conversation, writing a book or participating in a political campaign, is so rounded that its end is an end and not an end. Such an experience is a whole and carries with it its own individualising quality and self-sufficiency. It's *one* experience.

Are there hot or cold pictures and is that the same thing as saying that the pictures are emotional or not? Jean Baudrillard (2001:160) thinks that mediation makes everything feel like a media event. Think of a game of computer chess. Is the intensity coming from the chess game or the computer activities? One is about play, the other about playfulness. The same goes for a TV broadcast football match. Baudrillard thinks we shouldn't think it's about the same match: one is hot, the other cold – one is a game, with its emotional charge, its audacity and choreography, the other is tactile, modulated (play, close-ups, panning) , slow motion, different angles, etc.). The TV broadcast match is above all a TV broadcast event, such as the Holocaust or the war in Vietnam and can hardly be distinguished from the latter.

The experience of the picture goes very fast, writes Bo Bergström (2000:135). The experience of the image consists in part of a personal emotion and judgement, and in part an impression of the impression and a kind of response or reaction. It is this little drama that we constantly repeat and go through with each viewing of images. This means that every new image we see is not considered based on a void – we create the contexts needed to find any meaning in the image.

Baudrillard believes that the introduction of color television in the United States, which had been slow and difficult, gained momentum because one of the major networks decided to introduce color into television journalism. It happened during the Vietnam War and studies have shown that the "color gameplay" and the technical sophistication carried by this innovation provided images of the war that were gentler to show to the public. The "more" truth, the greater playful distance to the event. So we tend to appreciate what is wrapped up and the color's cosmetic subtleties. In this way, the misery seems at least colorful. The color helps to seduce us viewers.

The Holocaust is, says Baudrillard (2001:161), first and foremost (and only) a televised event (we must not forget Marshall McLuhan's basic rule: the medium is the message). That is, it is an attempt to heat a tragic but cold historical event, the first major event in the cold systems, cooling systems, deterrence and extinction systems that would then be deployed in other forms (including the Cold War, etc.) – and an event affecting the cold masses (Jews are no longer involved, but in the end they are forced to deal with their own death, the masses are no longer rebellious – discouraged by death, discouraged to death). A cold event is warmed by a cold medium for the masses, themselves cold, who will only experience a posthumous feeling, a tactile and dissuasive horror that allows them to slip disaster into oblivion with a kind of aesthetic good conscience.

The attempts to warm up all this and the political and educational orchestration that followed the televised event in an attempt to make sense of it were not excessive, writes Baudrillard. The panic of the program's possible consequences on children's minds, social workers mobilised to filter it, as if this artificial resurrection carried a risk of infection! In fact, the danger was the opposite –the one that results from social inertia of cold systems – cold that produces cold. Thus, the whole world must be utilised to reconstruct the social (heat) of communication from the cold extinction monster.

Brown and Phu (2014:10) argue that when photographers began to place higher aesthetic demands on their images in the mid to late nineteenth century, conservative critics criticised these efforts through an argument based on the camera's inability to capture the operator, the prospective artist's emotions. "Art", the argument goes, "does not depend on knowledge, but on emotion," as the English art critic Philip Gilbert Hamerton noted in 1887. To get the viewer to "love the work, an artist must win our sympathy with his emotions." As those familiar with the history of art photography know, it was the camera's indelible documentation of all the details, the apparent inability of the operator to choose one detail over another, which left the photographer outside the confines of art. With this view, the camera's "exact imitation of nature" prevents the artist's central role in making and communicating aesthetic judgments and results, following Stillman's polemics, "a photographic view can have neither emotion nor expression". The outlook was not more hopeful for the portrait. While portrait painters can capture the model's rising emotions and still retain them in memory to reproduce them faithfully, the camera's inability to capture such fleeting moments in the time of wet film photography meant that all photographic portraits necessarily became caricatures of the model's emotional life. As Hamerton argued, "photography is a purely scientific and insensitive art" – in other words, not art at all.

Photographs can achieve a status similar to that of a

religious icon – they are adorned, worshiped or worshiped, even in cases where the political beliefs of the depicted persons are anti-religious, Ilija Tomanić Trivundža (2014:223) states. After Che Guevara's death, the famous portrait of him became the object of religious worship (the portrait was taken to the church to be blessed and hung next to a picture of Christ and the Virgin Mary) and Mao Tse-tung's portrait became part of wedding ceremonies. What should be noted is that the belief in the "added value" of photographic portraits is maintained by idolaters and iconoclasts. Pictures of political opponents or former lovers are destroyed precisely because, at some level, people claim that the act of violence will in some way be transferred from the image. Also, "public demonstration" is an important aspect of iconoclastic acts, the truncation of images and the emotional intensity with which it occurs indicate the concept of the transmission of pain to the depicted person himself.

Regardless of the specific form of belief in "added value" in photographic images, the view expresses that the images have some form of inherent, almost enchanting power over the viewer. This special power can generally be interpreted as a power over the rationality of the human mind. We let ourselves be influenced, we let the emotions of photography into our own emotional lives.

The interpretation of the meaning of photographs is described by Allan Sekula (1982:85) as "incomplete statements", a message that "depends on some external matrix of conditions and conditions for its readability" Mitchell (2005:27) writes . Consequently, the power of photographs cannot be derived merely from their transparent immediacy, full of the potential to evoke feelings and desires, but also from their intangibility of definite meaning – images are powerful and magical because of their silence, because of "their stupid insistence that repeat the same message" which transforms them into blank spaces for projecting ideas. This projection is not limited to the meaning of what is shown in the image, but extends to our understanding of photography as a medium for preserving tracks, both "real" and "magical".

Protected middle-class residents in the more affluent corners of the world – the regions where most photographs are made and consumed – learn about the world's horrors primarily through the camera: photographs can and do create pain, writes Susan Sontag (1973:85). But the aesthetic tendency in photography is such that the medium that mediates anxiety ends by neutralising it. Cameras miniaturise the experience, turning the story into spectacle. As much as they create sympathy, photographs cut away sympathy, distancing the emotions.

The realism of photography creates a confusion about the real, which (in the long run) is analgesic morally, as well as (in the long and short term) stimulating the mind. Therefore, it cleanses our eyes. This is the healthy vision everyone has been talking about.

Sarah Parsons (2009:290) objects to that emotions are at the center of Sontag's famous, often frustratingly contradictory and incessantly exploratory book "On Photography" which is an attempt to understand the moral implications of the power of photographs that provoke strong emotions. Elsewhere in the text, Sontag argues that in order for photographs to link emotions such as those they received when viewing photographs from the Holocaust to morality and for those emotions to awaken conscience, viewers must already have a context to place them in. An important observation is that we do not understand photographs that we can not interpret or can put into a meaningful context for us.

"In the movie about the bullfighter Manolete we are present at the death of the famous matador and although our feelings may not be as deep as if we had actually been in the arena at the historical moment, they are of the same nature," writes André Bazin (1967:98).

What we lose by not being eyewitnesses ourselves, we cannot recapture because of the artificial closeness provided by the photographic magnification. Everything takes place as in the time and space that is the definition of presence.

Febvre and Bloch sought a new type of history that explored, in addition to the usual political history of states and kings, the social and economic structures of a society and its "mental tools", namely belief systems and collective emotions that people in the past understood and which made sense in their world, Alon Confino (2008:77-78) writes . This history of mentalities provided a whole new method for studying the past, as it took the history of collective representations, myths and images seriously. The story of the collective memory – of how societies remember their past, how they represent it and lie about it - was seen as an important part of this work. In 1924, Bloch published his classic "Les Rois Thaumaturges" about "beliefs and fables" around medieval royal healing rites, using terms such as "collective ideas" and "collective representations." In the mid-1920s, he began to use the term "the collective memory." What, then, is the collective consciousness? Is it about education or is it a matter of some kind of cultural capital?

Photography is a dream

All the photographs we make are largely about capturing a dream. A dream about the photograph that really conveys something to the viewer. Great ambitions and stereotypes are not the same as telling something in the photograph. Now I'm probably one of the photographers who uses the most stereotypes of all, but it's not a good idea just for that reason. By stereotypes I mean photographs of worn out people, pictures of children and animals. The list can be made longer. Someone wrote about this at one time that Western men with cameras tend to photograph "savages, women and children". The savages, who are not like us "Western men", because they seem dangerous, women because they are beautiful and children because they are cute.

The list of these stereotypical photographs can be made very long, that's no doubt. However, we all have the same opportunity to create something new, but we still tend to recreate things that have already been done.

Although it is not a matter of directly copying a document, the images we have seen affect our motives similar to the ones we have seen. It's probably about the image bank in our brain influencing us to make copies of images we have already seen others do. What we should do is to be inspired by the images already made to create new images, make sure something new is created.

The images we seek to capture are parts of a kind of dream we are trying to chase, something that we look for in all streets and squares. Something that we believe exists in everything we create, where we want to go to understand all the individual parts. Then it is, possibly, a part of ourselves that we try to take a photograph of outside in the reality we consider around us. Where we know it will cause us difficulties.

If it's as simple as making a photograph of something we imagined, it should be in the surroundings that give us a part of everything. We can basically see some kind of image in everything we see, we can give up the idea of a meaningful image and then suddenly we make a picture that fills us with wonder: have I managed to make this? What we cannot think we cannot understand. If we can't imagine that a worn alley in a sunny neighborhood can have "beautiful" components, we will never be able to take a photograph of the beauty. Susan Sontag (1973) said that we can see the beautiful in the ugly, because we do not really photograph the ugly, but chase the beauty of the ugly. If we can think of, and planning a photograph, the risk is striking that someone else has already made it. If I can figure something out, everyone else can do it too.

The photographic image can, by what may be called a dream, prove to the viewer as visual experiment if the viewer does not "understand" the photograph. When an image purely "objectively" contains two or more stories, it depends on which parts of the stories we manage to convey to the viewer. In this way we cut a kind of film of details, the light play and the characters' positions and looks – fragments of events in the photographs we capture. Here, chance can play a big role. Afterwards, when I look at the photographs on the big screen, I can see details I was not fully aware of at the time of exposure. I probably saw something, made a frame and pushed off. Here, this way is similar to photographing the literary cut-up techniques used by William Burroughs and also Bob Dylan. Several events, which may not be related, are in the same photograph and make it dreamlike, magical or mysterious.

In this way, the stories within the image get a depth that they may not have had about only what we initially reacted to when we exposed it. Randomly, or possibly our subconscious, saw details we were not immediately aware of and gave us the image that surprises us at the screen. However forced together, the stories in a photograph of this type are more complicated and therefore give "more" meaning, although perhaps not "better" meaning.

What then captures us in a photograph? Is it about the dreamlike or the hallucinatory? Or is it just the fact that the fast brain helps us to focus on a section of what we see? With the exception of how deep the focus we set, the camera does not make such selective action. The camera gives us a picture of what is in front of the lens. The dreamlike thing occurs when we, as a viewer, study our photographs and discover all the details we did not observe at the time of exposure. The photograph appears as a scene from a dream. Here are things we recognise, but also things we have never seen. It may surprise or annoy us (since the image is "disturbed" by details we have not previously observed). However, it is a matter of contributions to the photographic story that the photographer can never really direct.

Creating photography

What is a photograph? Is it a memory, an object (although digital technology unlocks the idea of photos as objects). Many kinds of materialities are contained in a photograph. What happens when we create a photograph? What happens to the person who creates photography? Are there "motives" that attract and call on us viewers? Are there any forces in photography that we do not yet fully understand, using W. J. T. Mitchell's question: "What do pictures really want?" Mitchell (1996) links to the mystical or magical with photographs that Ilija Tomanić Trivundža (2014:218) discusses – the mystical, the spiritual or the supernatural that has existed in the photographic image's appearance ever since the technology became known. Both popular and theoretical discourses on photography have, since the beginning, permeated photography with ideas of spirituality, mysticism and the supernatural. Photographic images have been attributed to properties beyond their mere ability to depict an object or scene: they have been regarded as seductive, dangerous, suggestive or enlightening, insinuating the presence or origin of mythical, magical or divine powers. Political actors and professionals in the media often talk about the power of images to influence individual perceptions and to mobilise or sway group thinking, a process in which the normal relationship is considered overwhelmed by emotion, of "added value" for the images themselves. What is this all about? Do the pictures have their own load of pieces from the reality they depict, or does the viewer load the photographs according to their own agenda? My own delight are pictures that are difficult to interpret, images that contain their own "riddle" as a variant of the content in the picture.

Mitchell (1996) remarks on the theoretical descriptions of photography that they often indicate a "deficiency" in the language to explain the visual, or give up their pursuit of meaning, the most notorious case of the latter concerning Roland Barthes, whose analytical semiotic apparatus capitulated in front of a family photograph in *Camera Lucida*. Pierre Bourdieu (1990:73-74) notes:

> *"Photography is considered a perfectly realistic and objective way of depicting the visible world, since photography has since been added to social uses that are considered" realistic "and" objective*".

This way of looking at photography is a supposedly documentary aspect, but what does it mean to us as we try to create a photograph? What are we doing in order to make a photograph to tell us something? What happens when we try to create a meaning or a mystery in our photographs with the help of the world around us? Is it even possible?

What does a photographic image say?

We are constantly encountering old phrases such as "a picture says more than a thousand words" pointing in one direction - the picture has strong conviction, but at the same time pictures are often accompanied by texts. How is this related?

The photographer and artist Man Ray observes in his autobiography that when he would give a lecture and got the proposal based on the old Chinese saying of thought: “A picture says more than a thousand words”:

“*In some way, I mixed the words together, perhaps intentionally subconsciously, and explained that a picture could convey a thousand words. Has anyone ever seen an image that was not accompanied by a headline or a piece of text? Even when the work was obvious, like the portrait of a young man holding a flower by an old master – when I looked it up in the catalog I read there: Portrait of a young man holding a flower.* “ (1974:431)

The typical photograph is often accompanied by a caption of the type that Man Ray reproduces above. If it is that the imagery is a means of communication on its own, it feels absolutely superfluous to attach captions as Man Ray tells us above. Various processes seem to be behind this general densification of images. At least since photography was invented, image types have constantly increased Göran Sonesson (1999:13) writes .

Generally, there are two ways to create an image: by hand, that is, usually with some simple instruments held in the hand, such as a pen, brush or sketch pen or by some more complicated mechanical device.

The first method can be called a chirographic method and the second a technographic or a mechanographic one. Examples of images made technologically are photographs, video films and the computerised graph. Generally, it takes much less time to produce a technographic image than a chirographic of similar size and complexity.

Furthermore, the technographic way of producing images is accessible to a much larger number of people, as it does not require the skill that takes a long time to learn or any innate talent. The criterion then applied is not to produce artistic images, but an elementary transfer of information about the represented object.

The history of image production in the West has also resulted in an increasing number of replicas (or copies), both in absolute terms and in relation to each type of image. Of course, it has always been possible to produce copies and since painting became a craft, the procedure has been of fundamental importance, as an educational process and a way of practicing the profession.

The mechanical techniques of reproduction make it possible to produce more and more copies that maintain the similarity to the original poster (which corresponds to the original or is at least one step closer to it). The image thus becomes a character more and more similar to the linguistic one, in the sense that each statement can now be repeated and remain exactly identical; in other words, in the sense that multiple copies can be made of the same type.

It is at this stage that a work of art, according to Walter Benjamin (1974), becomes mechanically reproducible, can generate many replicas. In this process, it probably loses its "aura", which is associated with its character of being unique, which is now highly valued.

The images we create with the help of a camera seem to fulfill several functions – documentation of our lives with pictures of children, relatives and various possessions and proof of our consumption. In that way, they naturally express a meaning in our lives and about our lives.

When we try to "create" (I prefer to avoid this pretentious word) photographic images that should contain the thoughts and ideas we have about life, love, work and death we end up in situations since we have been bombarded with images of throughout our life. Of course, this means that we have ideas about what a "sad" image is and what a "happy" image should look like. What we have to decide is if this is really about creating? Of course, a part of the creative process is about mimicking others to get a grip on how they have done to achieve their photographs.

During the time we spend making all these images that have already been made, and probably better than we can achieve, hopefully we will learn how to handle the tools and can give ourselves a try to make our "own" pictures.

If they are to differ from all the images we have consumed while we learned the craft, it is important to take in, perhaps to concentrate on a small area and dig down deep there.

Maybe it's about making ten thousand photographs of a dirt road during all seasons and lighting conditions we can handle. Maybe then we will succeed with a single really meaningful image. I usually expect to make a hundred exposures to get a decent picture, a thousand to get one that I can print on paper and ten thousand to get one I can consider to be good. Of course, it happens, but rarely, that I make three to four decent photos during a single afternoon. However, the hundred exposures are a rule that confirms the exception.

Susan Sontag (1973:4) argues that photographers, when deciding what an image should look like by preferring one exposure over another, force norms on the subjects. Although there is a sense in which the camera actually captures reality, not just interprets it, photographs are as much an interpretation of the world as paintings and drawings are. The occasions when photographs are relatively indiscriminate, promiscuous or self-effacing do not diminish the teaching throughout the process. This passivity – and prevalence – in every photograph is the "message" of the photograph, its aggression, notes Sontag. According to Sontag's view on photography, photography is a kind of exercise of power. The photographer decides what the current photograph is about.

Rosalind Krauss (1978:31) refers to the author Honoré Balzac's theory that all physical bodies as a whole are made up of layers of ghostly images, with an infinite number of leaves like skins, one on top of the other. Since Balzac believed that man was incapable of creating something material from a revelation, from something intangible – that is, to create something from nothing, he concluded that every time someone had made a photograph of him, one of the spectral layers was removed from the body and transferred into the photographic image. Repeated exposures meant the inevitable loss of the next ghostly layer, that is, the very essence of life. We know that people in certain cultures do not like being photographed. Some of the soul is taken away from the subject, in this view, which is very similar to Balzac's ideas above.

What do we want to say about photography?

The thoughts we put into the photograph we look at – do they belong in the photograph – or only in our own brains?

Can we see something in the photograph that we have not seen before? If we don't understand what we see, maybe we don't see anything? It could mean that in the photograph we see things that we recognise, or perhaps that leads us into the seemingly inescapable fascination with the exotic – that is, what we are not so familiar with.

These may include environments from other countries, less exposed environments at close range and people with different varieties of more, or less, exotic appearance. These environments as motives have, of course, been justified as documents for documentation. The question, however, is whether we see something in these motifs that the more everyday motifs do not give us? Or is it just a matter of motives that seem new to the viewer?

Exotic (new to us) can be the motives even if we use unusual angles, times and give us into it "new" images. Perhaps the most important thing is to see what we are getting into. Perhaps "exoticism" is merely an expression of seeing the world in new ways. The exotic may be hiding in our vicinity. It is enough for the first time to see a picture of yourself in profile – there is an exoticism there that is exciting – despite the fact that the subject is very close to ourselves. Then we may realise that the exotic is the new and hidden by the everyday. This could mean that we can, underneath the seemingly mundane, find motifs that fascinate other people than the photographer alone.

Then there is a tendency, besides taking new or good pictures, to basically make the same photograph time and time again. The motifs may appear to be different, but the composition and the cut out of reality is a repetition of images that the author has already made. It is reminiscent of what is said about some fictional writers – some write the same book again and again. Maybe this is the right way to go, to work on some kind of composition until you cannot extract more from it? In this way we milk a composition by implementing it on almost all motifs that come our way. It's about some kind of technology, or trick that has given us what we previously thought to be "good" image. So, we repeat the approach.

It provides, at best, increased competence or at least increased experience. By applying an invidious formula to the motifs, we become increasingly confident in solving what we believe photography should be about. Maybe we all just have a single image within us? The one that is the important image for us and therefore we tend, with some variations, to repeat it until we feel ready to throw ourselves into other motives? The ambitions a photographer may have are about what he is trying to find out in his surroundings.

Attempts to make the same image repeatedly can possibly be about recreating an image from the past in our lives. I notice that when I photograph children, which is rare, that I prefer scenes that remind me of my own childhood. This can be about angles, relationships between the child's size and the adults, or the children's positions in relation to surrounding buildings. There is something that I am probably in the process of working on. Since I am careful about photographing unknown children without accompanying parents, this project does not progress very fast. However, I see from some of my behavior in the image processing that there seems to be traces of the 1950s in it.

In all situations where we can make a photograph, the

likelihood is that today, with digital technology, we do. We may fathom that today in one day, as many photographs are taken as in the entire 1950s. The "bare foot photography" has grown so tremendously with this new technology, where even fairly cheap mobile phones have a 6 MP camera that can, under favorable circumstances, produce an image that is offset printable in A4 format. What does this mean for photo production and photo consumption over time? Is it possible to even guess what this will mean over time?

What happens when we make a photograph? Here is a list of some thoughts on this:

- The image is recorded on the media (film, plate or memory card)
- The image is processed (darkroom or image editing program)
- The image is saved (photo album, or digitally in album on some kind of hard drive)
- The image is displayed to others (possibly)

It may be deduced from the list above that digital technology has not led to any major changes in the workflow, or for that matter, the exposure of the photograph. The big difference is the ability to copy (clone) the image we want to deliver. Contrary to what the analog technology provided, digital technology makes it easy to distribute the image files without any loss of technical quality.

Despite all these steps, we may still ponder what photography really means. It's about capturing a moment, in some kind of subjective sense, and reading the image to spread it somewhere. Maybe it is just a trait in our own consciousness or in other people's consciousness. Is that what André Bazin (1967:14) puts forward, a way of the photographer to "embalm time", the underlying intention or intent of photography does not play a major role. Even the fairly experienced barefoot photographer may experience that certain things in the surroundings catch his eye. Why this particular motive and not another?

Susan Sontag claims in "On photography" (1973:65) that photography is not based on the ugly. Possibly from the beauty of the seemingly ugly. No one has ever discovered ugliness through photographs. But many have discovered beauty through photographs. With the exception of the situations where the camera is used to document or mark social rites, what makes people photograph is to find something beautiful. (The name under which Fox Talbot patented the photograph in 1841 was calotype: from *kalos*, beautiful.) No one exclaims: "It's so ugly, I have to make a photograph of it!". Even if someone said that's all it would mean: "I think the ugly thing ... is beautiful." Sontag connects to the motto of Marcel Proust, who begins this collection of texts: "The discovery journey does not consist in searching for new land but in looking with new eyes." (my translation). When we look around with fresh eyes, trying to see the beautiful in the seemingly ugly, we are about to find meaning in what seems to have none. However, it is quite possible that what I consider ugly is precisely what someone else regards as beautiful. With digital technology, we have every opportunity to constantly try to convince each other of the beauty of the seemingly ugly.

To enter the image into the text

Is it a bad idea to let the image exclude the words / text or force the text on a photograph? An image presented without a name, title or caption is possibly a different image than the one accompanied by text. I remember how at some magazines where I worked we talked about "inserting the image into the text", i.e. using a genre image and writing a caption to make that image appear as part of the text. It is unclear if it really worked. In any case, we made our valiant efforts to make it work.

Göran Sonesson (1989:8) points to an idea of Barthes'; the idea that any image contains information in itself or alternatively that it contains so much contradictory information that a verbal message is needed to determine its meaning. It has been noted that it was because of Barthes mainly studying highly organised communicative contexts, such as advertising and press photographs, that Barthes became convinced of the leading role of the verbal language even in the understanding of images; but neither photo art nor scientific photographs appear to be linguistically determined to a comparable extent, although their interpretation requires that they really be put into a slightly more general background frame, that is, equated to a selected set of interpretation systems defined by the particular Life World; but there is no need for these to be linguistic in nature.

The image is the model

The film theorist André Bazin (1967: 14) has said some wise things about the photographic image. I do not know how much he photographed, he was criticised for having a lot of views on movie production without having made film himself. Perhaps it is a basic requirement to have participated in the production – but it still seems that Bazin in his way of confronting the painted image with the photographic comes to some thoughts – maybe obvious, but interesting. Only a photographic lens, says Bazin, can give us the kind of image of the object that is capable of meeting the deep need that man has of replacing the need with something more than just an approximation, a kind of decal or transmission. The photographic image is the object itself, the object is freed from the conditions of time and space that govern it. No matter how blurred, distorted or discolored, regardless of how the image may be in the absence of documentary value, it shares, through the very process of its creation, the existence of the model of which it is a reproduction; it is the model. Hence the charm of a family album, Bazin says. These grey or sepia-toned shadows, ghost-like and almost indistinguishable, no longer traditional family portraits but rather the disturbing presence of life stopped at a certain point in time, freed from their fate; however, not with prestige art, but by virtue of a pristine mechanical process: photography does not create eternity, as art does, it embalms time, it simply saves it from its own past.

André Bazin thus says that photographic images preserve time, embalms it, we can see the time in photographs from yesterday and even further back. What this means to having to think about when creating a photograph, we shall return to.

What considering an image and the tactile experience means when we study a picture in a book have interested

Jean-Luc Nancy (2008:51). He uses the term *corpus*. A corpus is not a discourse and it is not a story. So a corpus is what we would need here. Here is a promise that this must mean that the body should be involved, almost immediately. A promise of the kind that is not the subject of a thesis or something to be quoted and recited or has the character of a story. In fact, a kind of promise to keep quiet. A silence that is less "about" the body than "from" the body, subtracts it materially from the meaning of its imprint and does so on the written and read page. Bodies touch each other, for good or bad, on this page, or more precisely, the page itself is gripping (my hand as it writes, and your hands as they hold the book). This touch is infinitely indirect, machines, vehicles, photocopies, eyes and additional hands are all pushed in - but it continues as a small, resistant, fine texture, the minimal dust of a contact, everything is interrupted and sought. In the end, here and now, your own eyes touch the same trace of signs as mine, and you me, and I write you. Somewhere this happens. This "somewhere" lacks the quality of a sudden transmission, as exemplified by the fax machine. In this way, the original touch or operation continues through every stage of a photograph's life.

What exactly is a photographic reportage, an image story, asks Henri Cartier-Bresson (1952:4-5)? Sometimes there is a unique image whose composition possesses such power and wealth and whose content so radiates outward from it that this single image is a whole story in itself. But this rarely happens. The parts that together can turn sparks out of a motif, often scattered – either in terms of space or time – and to bring them together by force is "stage management" and, I feel, cheating. But if it is possible to make pictures of the "core" as well as the sparks of the subject, this is a picture story and the newspaper page reunites the supplementary parts that are scattered in several photographs. Things-as-they-are offer such an abundance of material that a photographer must guard himself against the temptation to try to do everything. It is important to cut from the raw material of life - to cut and cut, but to cut with distinction. While he is actually working, a photographer must reach an exact awareness of what he is trying to do.

These kinds of choices that Cartier-Bresson describes are what happens with a kind of automation when our gaze is captured by any motive. First we don't see it, then we see it and then it's gone. Afterwards, we can only determine if we could possibly catch what caught our eye.

Susan Sontag (1973:67) argues that early photography came to change our view of reality – photography came with time to influence how we view reality – more or less as a photograph of the same. Released from the necessity of having to make narrow choices (as art painters did) about what the images were worth weighing because of the speed with which the camera depicted, photographers saw a new type of project: like seeing oneself, being conducted with sufficient vivacity and purposefulness, could actually unite the claims of truth and the need to find the world beautiful. When a wonderful object, because of its ability to register reality faithfully as well as disdained first for its basic accuracy, ended the camera by providing a tremendous promotion of the value of expression. Photographs not only represent reality in a realistic way. It is the reality that is being examined and evaluated, for its allegiance to photographs, Sontag says, quoting Émile Zola:

> "*In my opinion,*" Zola, the foremost ideologue in literary realism, explained after fifteen years of amateur photography, "*one cannot claim that have really seen something until you have photographed it.*"

Instead of just registering reality, photographs have become the norm for how things appear to us, thereby changing the very idea of reality and realism. Of course, there is a great deal in this line of reasoning. If I do not make a photo of the two-headed giraffe I say that I have seen, few will believe in my testimony.

Chantale Boulanger (1996:160-162) describes three levels of photography's way of communicating. *The first* is about the strength of the statement, the actual deposit. In the early 1980s, the discourse of photography was largely dependent on the idea of the photographic as a theoretical entity, for example a knowledge-theoretical category that introduced a report specific to the characters, the real, to do, to be, says Philippe Dubois in "L'Acte photographique" (Dubois 1983:58). The ontology of the photographic image is then redefined by what turned out to be a new category of thought. The photograph is no longer analysed as a single image, but as a truly iconic act. In other words, the gap between the product (finished message) and the process (action in progress) ceases to be relevant. *The other way* Chantale Boulanger describes as the iconic model. The criterion of equality helps to establish the snapshot as another place to investigate and take over.

The third way Chantale Boulanger brings up is "photographic writing". The photograph distances itself from reality to produce an image that is the shadow of reality; inside it opens a refraction which instead places the photograph as opposed to the one represented. Through this hole, which allows us to see the performance, the viewer experiences an ambiguity at heart. The iconic dimension appears as a double principle through it is a pleasure to look at, while we question the photographic representation where things are only in images that the photograph reflects. The interesting image presents a critical area, while providing a "super-coding that infiltrates impulses, passions and dream worlds". This image criticises the artistic, Boulanger (1996:163) writes, in contrast to Benjamin's cult image, as it provides a subjectivity that does not reduce photography to a technique for capturing and maintaining the presence of having-been-there. This icon really tells the story of a vision, as a subject that manipulates photographic gifts. The movement of the characters does not unilaterally make the world of images, but is often created by the artist's subjective intervention.

Clive Scott (1999:17) stresses two versions of what happens in contact with photographic images. Roughly speaking, the *first version* claims that photography "happens" when exposed, in visual contact with the world, as if it exercises the photographer's ability to see into his environment, to anticipate, to intuitively encounter revelation or significance in his surroundings. The *second version*, indicates that the exposure of the photograph is only a necessary bridge between the creative efforts in pre-photographic and post-photographic.

In this very first version, personal expression means responsiveness to the surrounding "dynamics", an empathy with what provides the observer with a special visual sensitivity to the subtle nuances and variations of the scene. Thus, personal expression lies in making an expressive image, not in any introduction of oneself on stage. In other words, "subjectivity" is not meant as selfishness in the process of acquiring the world but as a rare ability, seemingly passive, but which is in fact an active operative relationship with, or cooperation with, the living environment. The notion of the camera, reduced to a "sensitive plate", expresses this state of active accessibility to the environment. The art of the first version is mainly in sight and to benefit from chance. So we have the opportunity to observe and act in the way that the "thing" gives us a vision of seeing.

The second disturbance factor, writes Clive Scott (1999: 18), is the degree to which the photographer is identified by his subject (and therefore specifically reacted, prevented from seeing), or unidentified (and therefore free to see, to capture the spontaneous, but also intrusive, deceptive, voyeuristic). Nowhere is the dilemma bigger than in the highly moral universe of documentary photography. The ideal seems to be "identification as a photographer, but total social assimilation", a mix many photographers feel is achievable, but about which one can only be skeptical. Brassai in the underworld of Paris had typical ambitions:

"*But it was very difficult for them to overcome their distrust of me. Despite the owner's approval of the [popular ballroom], I was still an intruder in the eyes of some of them. What I wanted was that the proposal to photograph would not come from me, but from them. Some believe that a person's awareness of the photographic act provides an emotional exchange characteristic of it and valuable for that very reason.*"

According to this view, the characters in the picture form some kind of link to the photographer in the manner of photography, which differs slightly from traditional street or sports photography, where the person in the picture is usually not aware that the picture is taken.

Jonathan Crary (1988:29) argues that the emergence of photography and film in the nineteenth century is an end product of a long chain of technological and / or ideological development in the western world when camera obscura develops into the photographic camera. It is understood that at each stage of this development, the same basic assumptions about the observer's relation to the world have been made.

Does the chance of making a "good" image increase when making many exposures?

On the one hand, it seems like chance would help us get at least one good image if we snap a thousand exposures. On the other hand, it may be that the person who makes many pictures eventually gets better at making pictures. There are examples of photographers who make few exposures and there are examples of those who waste their exposures. Both approaches work, it seems clear.

Maybe a relatively large number of exposures provides more opportunities for chance to come to the photographer's assistance? If you do not practice in the foreign languages studied, such as English, French and German, they will not get better. They temporarily get worse, but they repair quite quickly when used. Is it similar to photography that it functions as a language, part of the so-called "imagery" we sometimes hear about? If we use our knowledge, it may be easier to put it into something that others can see benefits in. Therefore, I use the analogy with spoken languages. It is through exercise that we become better at everything we do. Part of that exercise may be the number of exposures and exposure opportunities. The photographic image writes its meaning with light and that is the light we try to capture when exposing. It gives an impression of the medium we catch it on. Compared to the "saved" memory, photography is more permanent or unchanging, but compared to the written word there is a fairly even competition be-tween text and image. Text and image are, in a certain manner, perhaps competitors, but may even be regarded as collaborative partners.

Although some photographers insist on writing captions for their photographs, this is probably because they do not trust their photography, or as a way of pointing out a charge that all viewers might not deduce from the image themselves. However, the caption locks the viewer on an interpretation and that may be the author's intention, but I like the "open" images more where all viewers are given the opportunity to do their own reading of the photograph. Man Ray (1974) was a critic of captions and captions, he claimed that they did not add anything. The caption for a photograph is like calling a text "novel" or "essay", this label limits the viewer to fewer interpretations, which means a greater effort to get out of it than to "interpret" the original image without the attached text.

We may need those cues, or our reading will be hampered by them and become more rectified and single-minded. Something that we no longer need in the world of rectified commercialism, where everything is merchandise that is primarily "for" commerce and not experience.

Stories in a photograph are stories in the photograph and not in a caption or title. There even some of the best photographers go askew. Of course, they have a story in their image, but they obviously don't trust it enough to let it act on its own, but create a caption to send the story in the viewer's direction.The question is if the viewer needs that help? The image should be able to stand on its own feet without help. If the author is doubtful as to whether there is any content in the image at all and must reinforce it with a caption, it is an argument between the image and the author. In some cases, of course, a caption or title may be justified, but at the time of writing I find it difficult to determine which cases it would be. If the image is to be able to act on its own, the advice to the caption author is: remove the captions / titles from the photograph for a while. You will realise that they are not needed – the story's agency acts on its own without the need for support from text. The photographic image also becomes much freer in its design of the story's design and embraces the world and the story in a new way.

Whatever you do with the caption or title, the most important thing is that you present the "naked" image. Continue with that, so the use of the caption as support wheel for the photograph may disappear over time.

The photograph is a depiction

Although photographs are objects in themselves, at least when they appear in a viewable state in front of the viewer, they exist in their function as images of something in the rest of the physical world. They may say something about that world or they won't. However, it is important to remember that photographs are those images. It is usually as such that they are presented to the beholder's eye. This is a picture of a thing, a house, a person or a bridge. We keep making pictures of something and we may never let what the image tells us to expand the story we let it tell.

On the one hand there is a story we try to get by composing pictures and possibly some image processing on it. However, sometimes the image seems to live a life on its own and have its own story that takes over the one we are trying to attribute to it.

Then it doesn't matter how much we have composed. The image has its own story. Probably it was the one that drew us to try to make this picture, but we didn't see the "real" story, but saw some other version of it that got us started.

But who knows? There may be more than this main story to study. Maybe we've just seen the beginning of the stories yet? Probably there are far more stories in the image than we can imagine. So we have to do just that: first write a story in the image in a way that makes the image easier to grab for the viewer.

We can just keep trying to find that story and make an image of what it looks like. Hopefully, over time, we will get better at finding the stories we are facing. This is mostly about seeing the stories that are out there and partly creating their own stories based on that material. We cannot add anything more than our own creativity. There must be a basis for the story, otherwise it doesn't matter how good a photographer you are. The pure image, which all photography is basically about, is about bringing some of the theatricality or surrealism into the reality we interpret. It is there and it is through its elements, or at least some of them, that we create a dramatically imaginative photograph.

We must not forget that photography is a depiction of something and it is an image of a story even though we may have got it that it is a still image of a story and it is an extract from a story from the physical world that we captured and thus is part of reality.

If the photograph is an image, then a question rises: is it possible for it be independent? The answer will be both yes and no. The photographer's story only arises when the viewer takes possession of it. Then the viewers read all their ideas into what the photograph in question tells us. Everyone who views the photograph will see their own story that they can reproduce. Or as they think the photograph reproduces. Naturally, it is because they are different people.

They thus see different stories in that photograph and there is nothing strange about this. However, one should become suspicious if all viewers present the same story. The image is present and under consideration it appears. The image the viewer can see gives a reflection of what they see and that viewer tries to give hope of being able to absorb the "message" contained in the image and it is from the viewer's own thoughts that they recreate that message.

The image comes – only we take on that story in the outside world may feel more secure if we enter into this hunt with the firm assurance that it will be able to image that again. Probably it will be a different story then, as time has passed since the last time we studied the image and it now in parts becomes another. It may be reminiscent of the first, but here is another story and there should always be. It would be very surprising if we came back twice with an image that tells the same story.

Street Photography Continues a Tradition of the 'Flaneurs'

Street photography is about capturing snapshots in any environment – the thing about street is not the most important thing, but it is all about an environment with traces of people. Approaches and technology are about capturing people's lives in the picture, experiencing and capturing the moments through the camera. Street photography is a spontaneous photographic form in which the photographer, during his excursions in urban (mostly) environment, captures fleeting moments. One of the most well-known figures in cultural theory is the flaneur, who is analysed by Walter Benjamin, writes Haggerty & Ericsson (2000:605). The flaneur is a creature from nineteenth-century Paris who absorbs himself in walks through the metropolis where he is engaged in a form of urban detective work. Invisibly hidden in the crowd, the flanuer follows his fantasies to explore the streets and arcades to excavate the meaning of the urban landscape. In this formulation, we recognise the relationship between the street photographer and the flaneur.

The photographic image as the fourth wall

Occasionally, I make street photographs that appear to be taken in a theater scene. Then photography works as what in the theater world is called the "fourth wall", that is, the imaginary wall on the theater stage that looks out towards the audience. In the movie world, the camera acts as the fourth wall. The camera is where the intended viewer (and the photographer) moves in a scene from a play that is played in front of the camera's lens. Of course, the biggest difference to theater is that the photographer is mobile and the viewer can be too. However, these are the premises that the stage set called the "photographic image" has. What we see through the fourth wall is the place where the stories of photography are played out. As we try to access the deeper parts of the stories of the images, we try to penetrate the fourth wall and reach into the essence of the photographic image.

Some days when I am out making photography in the city it feels like I am looking at the world through a square tube. Suddenly I see something that resembles a story and snap a shot. Sometimes it becomes an image that I am reasonably satisfied with, and for the most part I wonder why I bothered to make an image – since I do not really understand why my attention was initially caught.

This also applies to all the scenes we pass that contain actors, or that I prefer to call them figurants, because they do not play but live their lives, whether or not I aim the camera at them. Especially in street photography, all the figurines are part of my experience. In all those scenes there is a kind of acting, which is really about the fact that figurants continue their lives as usual while I photograph them.

The photographs convey stories from the lives of others, but since it is I who "made" the photographs they are also part of the story of my life. These stories coincide and become the show that goes on around me, without interruption. Maybe I will become part of the show in this way or not, it depends entirely on chance.

The photographer, I, may consider himself a node in a network of events, scenes or maybe we call them stories. The network reaches via *figurant* and photographer all the way to the vernissage of the photographs in a gallery, or the presentation in a book. The viewers who show up there encounter a symbiotic story. Here are parts from the subject (figurants), the photographer and the viewer himself, which result in the stories that this viewer encounters via the exhibited photographic images.

In the gallery there are often other viewers and their possible comments can also be experienced as part of the story our viewers believe they receive from the photographic images studied. It is not an entirely uncomplicated event and there are also parts of this event that contradict each other.

It is about a complicated event in the gallery where we may encounter the photographic image as a piece in a play where it is hanging on the wall. One show tells us about the gallery, another about the show that went on when the photograph was made, another one is the experiences that the viewer gets from the photographic image plus the gallery when viewed. There are many stories waiting to be invented and none of them have any particular power over the others, but they rush into the viewer's consciousness when they are strong enough – together, or individually. It is an "experience" among others. This experience works like rings on the water, even though they carry on individual stories they become more interwoven than that. In a way, they create each other. If the viewer starts to defend himself, the rest of what we can call the main story of the viewer's life will soon begin and create a kind of sense of increased meaning. The story of the world continues in the mind of the viewer as the story manages to penetrate the fourth wall.

Henri Cartier-Bresson (1952:18) wrote in "The Decisive Moment":

> *"For me, photography is a simultaneous recognition, at the fraction of a second, of the importance of an event, but also an exact organisation of the forms that give the event its correct expressions. This can be said about almost all photography, but it is about taking a firm look at interesting and exciting, but also beautiful pictures of the fleeting moments that together create the urban street environment. In this way, the street photographer reflects everyday life."*

Cartier-Bresson's book "*Images à la sauvette*" was translated into English by the publisher and was called "The Decisive Moment" which cannot really be said to capture the meaning of the phrase "Images à la sauvette" which is closer to "Pictures made in flight" or "Sneaky pictures". The French phrase points towards Cartier-Bresson's preference for hidden, or spontaneous, photography contrary to what the English translation indicates. Pointing to the "decisive moment" as specifically for street photography is not so productive, but pointing out that it is about images made during flight indicates part of the nature of street photography. The decisive moment includes all photography, directed or not. It feels most like a platitude, who wants to publish the image that missed the "crucial moment"? Cartier-Bresson pointed with the term "images à la sauvette" towards the instantaneous and unregistered appearance in street photography. Today, there are many kinds of street photos – everything from what follows the idea of capturing images in flight to informed subjects who are asked to pose for a picture. The latter borders more on documentary photography.

Street photography is all about the "small events" – a look, a gesture, a mime, a hand that touches another or the light's play over a rain-wet pavement. The crucial thing is that street photography tries to record what the eye, and the camera, sees of human activities in the urban environment. Architecture is a foundation for all this, but in my opinion there must be people or temporary traces of people in the images. Architecture, in its perpetuity, constitutes an overly permanent trace of man to function on its own. It may be about lost clothing or possessions, but mainly people in the picture.

A street photograph does not have to include a stranger from the front, close up with a flash, something that, for example, the American street photographer Bruce Gilden does. Street photography can also be a backdrop of people. Now it should be said to Bruce Gilden's defence that he also makes "kinder" street photographs of dogs and the like.

The activity of the eye creates a prerequisite for photography

Walter Benjamin (1983:38) argued that relationships in large cities are characterised by a marked overweight of eye activity compared to ear activity. His explanation of why this is so is about the urban development of infrastructure in the form of transport. Before the development of buses, railways and trams in the nineteenth century, people had never had to look at each other for many minutes or even hours without talking to each other. Now they spend maybe an hour each day staring at their fellow travellers as they make their way to their workplaces.

The newcomers saw, according to Benjamin, people they had never met before passing through the streets, the workers of the industrial revolution generally came from the countryside where you recognised everyone you met, perhaps even knew their name and where they lived. In the city everything was different and although the noice must have been noticeable to the newly arrived, perhaps Walter Benjamin is entitled to a part in the visual impressions considered. In this way, the urban environment is a visual environment that contains many people, who through their presence trace further visual details.

Strolling among the people on the street, as viewers gliding around the rubble on the sidewalks, the wide streets and avenues that were developed after Baron Georges-Eugène Haussmann's redevelopment of Paris 1853-70, was something that poet Charles Baudelaire, among others, took to his heart – being a flaneur also became one of the driving forces for his poetry. Along history, time was created, the modern world was emerging, with the transformation of society at large. The poet Baudelaire was able to study the impact of the upheavals on the individual and to interpret what he saw in words.

The poet Charles Baudelaire for the first time made the city of Paris the main character in lyrics, writes Walter

Benjamin (2008:104):

"*This poetry is no hymn to the homeland; rather, an allegoric's gaze, as it falls on the city, is the alienated man's gaze. It is the look of the flan, whose lifestyle is still hiding behind an attenuating glory from the coming destruction of big city dwellings. The flaneur is still on the threshold of the metropolis, as well as the middle class. None of them have him in his power yet. He belongs in no camp. He seeks refuge in the crowd.*"

This location, on the eve of the metropolis or middle class, worked for the Flaneur-poet as the no man's land where he could more or less undisturbed study the folk life that took place before his eyes. Here are people on their way to meetings, workplaces, going on errands, going to meet lovers or about to rob someone.

The urban space basically acts as a theater scene. While participating in the theater play that is being performed all around them, citizens are part of the audience at this performance. Also, parts of the rural space, outside a grocery store or other place where people gather, will also be a possible place to make street photography. This despite all the absence of streets and urbanity.

Street photographers continue this tradition of viewing with the difference that they catch glimpses of what is happening on their film, or in modern times, on their memory cards. However, I notice myself that it is not easy to free yourself from all the images I have seen. It is easily done that the photographs made by individual photographers appear in thousands of versions, or clones.

Pierre Bourdieu (1990:75) writes in "*Photography: a*

middle-brow art" that the average photographer takes the world as he sees it, that is, according to the logic that belongs to a view of the world, with categories and a canon, which belongs to the art of the past. Images that, with the help of technical possibilities, break off ever so little from the dry academic vision of ordinary photography, are received with surprise. So, the pictures made in the street photography tradition may be more traditional than the technological development could make possible. Of course, it is easy to explain that we are all children of the world we grew up in and live in, we are shaped according to prevailing patterns and realise that it will eventually become difficult to break out of our habitual patterns.

Photographer Henri Cartier-Bresson writes about his experience of years of photography on the street when he notes:

"*For me, photography is a simultaneous recognition, at a fraction of a second, of the importance of an event, as well as an exact organisation of the forms that give the event its proper expression.*
I believe that it is through the act of life that the discovery of our own self is continually made with the discovery of the world around us that can shape us, but which can also be influenced by us. A balance must be established between these two worlds – one within us and one outside us. As a result of a constant reciprocal process, these worlds will form a single. And it is this world that we must communicate." (1952:18)

Cartier-Bresson seems to speak of a fleeting moment

where the intrinsic meaning of an event manifests itself, which means that the photographer must use his camera to capture that difficult subject. To some, not all viewers can agree on the meaning.

The British photographer and linguist Clive Scott (1999: 19) tells us that he made his photographs for a long time in stealth; that is, made them without anyone he was making pictures. It's really just the next best thing, Clive Scott argues, and says that no matter how daunting it may seem, it's always preferable to confront the person you're photographing. Since it is a good thing for the snapping of the image itself that it is somehow reflected in the face or attitude of the subject: such as surprise, anger, fear, amusement or flattered vanity, or obscene or provocative gestures.

The French Jesuit Michel de Certeau (1984:93-94) is interested in perspectives, he visits the World Trade Center and looks down on the city and thinks he is learning other things about the city below with this perspective. He sees the ordinary practitioners of perspectives in the city live "down there", below the thresholds at which visibility begins. They are walking – an elemental form of this experience of the city; they are hikers, whose bodies follow this urban "text" wind, which they write without being able to read it. We must remember that the text also stands for what we call image in everyday life. What de Certeau was aiming to show is that the viewer's perspective, both physical and mental, is very important when considering the world – and thus, even photographic images.

These perspectives are important when, like Clive Scott (1999:126), one thinks that a first argument for preference in a mute relationship with photography is simple, but perhaps not sufficiently emphasised: photographs are not just moments out of time, they are moments of contact with reality, even if reality is ending and may be geographically distant. Here Scott sees the volatility of photography, the kind of memory that a photographic image might be and recreate in the mind of the viewer. So it is not just about fragmentary pieces from our past, but more about a kind of light flashes that make contact with the past.

Clive Scott sees that in some way, over time and space, visual dialogue is possible; somehow this figure, with this look, is not disqualified by its past, not turned into a human preparation or historical document. It is the very feeling of the past in the picture that creates the magic of the contact. We travel back through the picture, to the time when it was made. This journey makes words inadequate, because they can give little justice to the image, they cannot do justice to the magic, because it is magic that makes words inadequate for her knotted fingers on the threshold, pulls the door closed, to the folds of the her coat, to the clarity of her image compared to the faces seen through the immense glass of another world out of reach – but a world she is about to become a part of – to the light that catches the door's hinges and so on.

According to Clive Scott (1999:126), the language is driven away by the photographic image. Our surprised discovery of these things, our desire to look at them again, to visually feel them without mediation, drives the language away. It is the intervention of language that would assign the image to a different time and place, free us from emancipation, interrupt the visual dialogue, transform the woman (in the image) into a social identity. The eye, handed over to its own units, lets its curiosity become a fascination, which explanation and interpretation would put an end to. Titles are crucial in this; they can either whisper discreetly and withdrawn, create magic or whine continuously so that magic can never establish itself. But here the indexicality creates a confirmation of a distance in time and space, which the title confirms with its careful notes, 05:30, 1978 and Medborgarplatsen, while also disproving the title by investing what has become ironic with an acute presence. The second argument for a mute relationship is closely related to the first and has to do with the very quality of the image, where Clive Scott concerning quality means what the quality of print can only enhance, sharpen and selectivity of focus, sensitivity and expressiveness in transitions and silence, or the "cool" that these things can communicate. The mute would then be proportionate to the extent to which photography realised its own "photographicity" where, by "photographic", we mean a new ocular physiology, a reconfiguration of the perceptual possibilities in the eye.

Clive Scott believes that photography conducts its own types of visual "accuracy" focused on sharpness, in black and white photography the ability to shed light on the subject with such care, which saves the most subtle gradations of tone, to delineate objects and different areas of the subject, with such clarity that these things exist with an eerie vivacity, they appear to have very strong reasons for being there. These qualities of photography can be referred to by language but not inhabited by it, since language is focused on human perception. Just as avant-garde music can try to rejuvenate the ear with sound through distinctive character – how descriptive is a distinctive character? – rather than the other way around, photography tries to update the vision and urges the image to project perception, rather than the other way around. Photographic gaze, perhaps again under the influence of painting, was domesticated before it was fully understood, treated as nothing more than an extension of camera obscura (does not see pictures, but fixes them); language has only continued this state. Arguing for the silence of photography is, if nothing else, necessary as a polemic gesture for the media's account of the non-recuperability of "innocent" images, of a social institutionalisation (of function, genre, etc.) that semiologises photography before it has had a chance to assert their photographicity, not as a code, but as a sensory experience.

Clive Scott's (2007:126-128) third argument relates, appropriately enough, to Barthes's closely intertwined arguments about a third meaning, the blunt meaning and the punctum. These conditions refer to picture elements through which the viewer is inexplicably pierced, wounded, affected and whose value or power appears to be directly proportional to the language's inability to anticipate or translate them. One aspect of the third meaning concerns our second reason above: it is a manifestation of the innermost being of the medium in question, the cinematic in the film, the photographic in the photograph, which, in the case of the latter, further defines Barthes as "having- -been ". But the third meaning is also a "signifier", hence the difficulty in calling it "my reading",

Barthes says. So the third, blurry meaning is punctum, complementary, probably disturbing, opening up the image to a subversive blind field. Although the trigger in the third sense is in the image, it belongs more to the viewer, annoyed by himself, than in the image itself. What, to me, can be the storage of forgotten memories, fantasies, names or psychophysiological associations? Punctum is the way in which, ironically, Barthes is capable of rescuing the intuitive from the throat grip of semiology.

Henri Cartier-Bresson, French street photographer, says:

"*Sometimes you have the feeling that you have already taken the strongest possible picture of a certain situation or scene; yet you experience how you compulsively squeeze, since you cannot be sure in advance exactly how the situation, the scene, will develop. You have to stay in the scene in case the parts of the situation protrude from the core again. At the same time: also avoid shooting like a shotgun and burdening yourself with useless documents that increase the clutter in your memory and destroy the accuracy of the report as a whole.*" (1952:5)

This is a fine description that Henri Cartier-Bresson makes of being on the move as a street photographer – trying to capture the fleeting happenings of relationships, statements and events that take place in the street. This – being in the fourth wall of the street spectacle – is almost in the spectacle, but a little outside the stage it is crucial to be able to make pictures of everyday fleeting moments.

American anthropologist Edward T. Hall (1990:134) portrays an understanding of the need for distance where

Germans appear to differ from Americans. During his research, Hall instructed students to photograph both a man and a woman in various contexts in public places. One of his assistants, who happened to be German, photographed his subjects from a long-range focus because: "*You are not expected to look at other people in public places because it is intrusive.*" This, Hall says, can explain the basic idea behind the German laws against photographing strangers in public places without their permission.

We know that the legislation in some countries, including Germany and France, differs from the open legislation we have in Sweden – where, basically, everything is allowed to be photographed in public – even the people who are there. The exception is certain protection items.

Photography as hunting

Certainly, we have at some point thought that photography in the urban environment has great similarities to what we think hunting for game in the forest means. Andrea Maria Dusl (2014:245-247) notes that hunting together with gathering is one of mankind's oldest cultural techniques. In its original sense, hunting means a planned search, capture and killing of animals, says Andrea Maria Dusl. Hunting as a basic human experience extends far beyond its function as a source of acquisition of food and materials. In addition, it may assume material and sexual nature. People chase each other in games, chase after the fleeing enemy, chase objects of sexual desire and even intangible as information or knowledge-hunting. Without empathy with the hunted, without foresight, without insight into their behavior, it is impossible to pursue a successful hunt. The history of domestication of wildlife would be unthinkable without this ability in humans. In the field that these forces span, something like hunting photography is possible. Man can, in connection with games, chase one another without killing each other. This usually means that both hunters and prey achieve a victory, Andrea Maria Dusl argues.

Maybe it is this playful component, writes Dusl, who is equally worthy of the photographers and the subjects photographed. The pursuit of the motif is physically harmless but not necessarily aggression against the motives recognised by fellow human beings. The booty is not the hunting object either, but his image, the portrait is the hunting object. The well-known image of hunting as a deadly ending occupation hides the fact that this is not the most photographed person (or persons) being hunted, but the photographed image of them – more precisely: Hunting is the moment when the image of the person may be retained and consequently also recorded.

Unlike in the hunt for animals, after the image, the killing or the deadly wounding of the object is not completed, the effect is not a "shooting", it can be repeated – and it is the image. The shot does not necessarily represent the end point of the hunt. The shot object can always be shot again without losing its vitality and individuality. The communication with the subject can be free of aggression, loving – and yet in line with the hunt for an image of him. The traditional "light painting" is perceived as passive, the photographer's observation role should be changed with the help of cameras with flash. The mobility of photographers now equals that of the hunter. The sudden and noisy release of a camera flash is reminiscent of the sound of a firearm being fired. The photographer's vocabulary has been expanded with the concepts of "shooting", or "exposing".

Susan Sontag (1973:10) explores in her polemical essay "In Plato's Cave" the dark aspects of hunting photography (or: photographic hunting) and notices the comparison between the camera and "robbery weapons" in everyday photography. "Just pull, aim, shoot," she quotes an ad for the camera Yashica Electro-35 GT. The manufacturer assured its customers that photography was as simple as firing a firearm.

Since the camera is a sublimation of the weapon, states Andrea Maria Dusl (2014:246-247), photographing someone is a sublimated murder. Important aspects of hunting (and therefore also of hunting photography) is that it is planned and practiced. Compliance with technical and craft rules, but especially the exact knowledge (possibly even careful reading) of "change" and terrain in weather and light. The planning of the hunt, the "shooting" not only has strategic components, but also sets a time frame. We can all sense when we "got" the picture we were looking for, but also when we missed it. The fast-passing moment when the spectacle on the street took place can quickly be turned into something completely different – and what was exciting is no more.

Henri Cartier-Bresson can also be said to have a hunting motive when he describes his way of working. Cartier-Bresson's book "Images à la sauvette" was translated into English and was called "The Decisive Moment" (1952) which cannot quite be said to capture the meaning of the phrase *"Images à la sauvette"* which is closer to "Pictures made in flight" or "Sneaky pictures". The French phrase points to Cartier-Bresson's preference for concealed photography, contrary to what the English translation indicates. With the term "images à la sauvette", Cartier-Bresson wants to point to the instant in street photography. Today, there are many kinds of street photos – everything from following the idea of capturing images in flight to directed subjects that are asked to pose for an image.

The location in the photographic image

Does it matter at all where a photograph is made? I mean it does in a special case and that is if it is about documentary photography in the sense that applies to, for example, police investigative work. Then there is reason to note at what exact location a photograph is made. Otherwise you can imagine that it is as with the caption, it is not something that adds anything to the viewer's experience.

It is more rewarding for the viewer's intellect to wonder at a conscious level: is it Paris or is this photograph made in Svedala, Sweden? When we ascertain (in a title or caption) that the photograph is made in Södertälje, we have taken the interpretative preference from the viewer and try to force her into something we as authors have devised. Showing a photograph of people in rush hour in a city center and giving it the title: "Evil at large, Amsterdam" does not turn on the viewer's thinking. We have already fixed it in a special compartment where we believe it should stick. For the viewer's, it is much more evolving to create their own experiences and to interpret their own stories within the picture.

We are diluting that difficulty by creating titles such as "Fall image, Paris" for our images, which means that we will never catch the interest of a completely unprepared viewer. "Paris, okay, but I don't like Paris". In this way, there is a great risk that the viewer's interest will be removed from the experience of the story in that picture. Probably we all want "hooks" to hang our thoughts and interpretations on, but we should not give the viewer too many cues, they will not help at all. We should never try to control how the viewer should regard our photographs. We can only try to capture the viewer's interest with the image we show. If we and the viewer have common references to geographical locations, the place in our photograph will be within the viewer's interpretation.

Otherwise, the geographical references will not appear or the viewer will create his own reference that works with the photograph and what is told in it. Whether or not the viewer recognises the place is part of the story, but it is not the whole story. It becomes easy if we specify the geographical location. By not entering it, we avoid shutting out some viewers and including others.

Now, of course, we can claim that we do not include the one who loves Paris, of course, but if you consider a picture stated to be made in Paris, it may not be the picture story in the first place that you are interested in. You want to watch postcards from Paris and there are an abundance of them. We don't have to create that many more photographs of the same thing. There are just enough people there are.

This makes it clear that the photograph has a place in

itself, but we do not need to give a written account of what we think it is. If we leave this to the viewer, everyone will feel so much better. Then I include the photographer, the viewer and the story of the photograph. When we mix text and image, something other than a photograph and its "captured" story arises, which in the beauty of its story can change lives. Then you do not want to tarnish the photograph with categories, descriptions or ethnic specifications about how the photograph came about. Aperture-life has its time, but you don't want that as a caption for your image.

These comments about the appearance of a photograph have their given place. When you compile a book with some of your pictures you can discuss in a separate text how you worked, how you made the photographs and so on. Save that information until then!

As soon as you can, you should stop describing photographs in text; stop trying to push your image theory into captions or find "nice" titles like "Inferno IX". It is not these details that propel the story of photography. The story of the image drives itself with each additional viewer.

Without the story in the photograph, your image is dead, so why are you trying to give the artificial breath support with captions and titles?

Narrative surrealism

Is it that surreal being caught in the moment that makes sense in a street photo? Henri Cartier-Bresson, who according to many is the father of modern street photography, was, according to Jackie Higgins (2013:44), influenced by surrealist artists and this contributes to a possible explanation of some of his photos. They are often about capturing moments in flight and thus preserving something that the viewer can then marvel at. Maybe purely documentary photography can play a role, but the little detail that makes the image an Image requires something completely different. Here is a detail that captures the viewer – Roland Barthes 'Punctum' (1993) if you wish.

Higgins (2013:73) also points out that the unexpected, like when an individual moves his arm unexpectedly at exposure, can help make a photograph more exciting. It may not be portrait-like or the photograph the author intended to make, but such a portrait points to the surreal that lurks amongst the reeds of everyday life. There, many abyss is hidden by scams where everyday life turns into drama, perhaps even without those who figure in the image knowing that they are in and creating this just by continuing their lives as usual. Everyday theatricality, the "caught in flight" thinking with Cartier-Bresson, may be about luck, about chance, but the most important thing is that the author was in this place at this specific moment and that the photographed persons. The photographer made the image at this very moment, which may never return.

The "proper light" and the simple boldness mean that photographs made in Swedish municipal communities appear to be exposed in French small towns shortly after the Second World War. It assumes that they are made as black and white images, but it is nevertheless fascinating that the boundaries are not so far away, neither to the past, to the geographical nor to the theatrical. With the "right" house from the last turn of the century, it is only a matter of seconds until the time travel starts. If the images emanate from a reality, we can never understand that we have experienced it in some other way. If what we do is part of something much bigger than what we imagine, does this mean that this image qualifies for the archives where they mainly store their photographs, or is it just a product of an epigone? An impersonator?

The thoughts we get by looking at a photo are probably a lot about seeing things we can "recognise", that is, we see patterns because we humans are good at it. If there is no such regularity, we are out on thin ice and waiting until someone else makes a judgment. Better to do that than to end up in a situation where we seem to be on the wrong track.

So, can no images that are unlike any other be "good"? At least for someone? Although they resemble something else, a childhood memory, a dream or a daydream. We are often rehearsing the most elementary of our lives, and it is these repetitions that give us those cocky convictions that this is "good" – that is "bad".

The "unusual" combinations of details in the image sometimes make them surreal, sometimes not. However, there is a chance that they will win this. Just photographing something that "deviates" from the norm is not the only thing that determines whether a photograph gets a surrealistic tone. Photographing worn-out alcoholics on a park bench does not provide a photograph with a story in itself, it is mostly about documentation. We would like to see cracks, shifts in the concept of time, something that gives shivers in our minds. Where are there mismatches?

A photograph of a worn out drug addict next to a prudent

gentleman in strict trench coat might create the tension needed to create a story in the photograph. To increase the clarity of the story, the looks and gestures of those who figure in the photograph are also needed. Documenting alone does not reach very far, as the image is very similar to other images made by other people and it is not sufficient when we show the image to people outside the immediate circle of friends. It is very important that you are given the opportunity to access the position required for you to be able to make the image that will be important. Here it is decided whether the photograph will be "good". You have to let your photograph tell those stories that the viewer has not yet called to life.

Without story, the exposure of the image is an exposed box among others and is only of interest to those most mourning. All others of us move on to the next picture.

Who decides on photography?

One of the more sensitive questions for all modes of expression is who decides, who has the privilege of interpretation when we want judgments about whether a photograph is "good" or not.

I can imagine a photo I made is good, but if no one else thinks like me it is a problem. Am I like Vincent van Gogh who only sold a couple of paintings to his brother and was considered a master only after his death, or am I just a dabbler in general? Is it the person who does not find any content, any technical skill or decent composition, who is entitled to judge my work? Or should it be the person who likes all the images he / she sees just because it's photographs? The answer is, of course, that none of them should evaluate my images. They may like whatever they like about the photos, but it is only you who decide which of those images you show to others.

Even if you are uncertain, never trust anyone else in terms of knowledge or taste. You have to decide for yourself if you can listen to all the others who offer their views, but it is not up to them to decide if the images you present are "good or bad". Compared to what? Compared to what other photographers have done? Who does the comparison? Remember that it's up to you all the time. There are far too many influential small popes within most industries and it is really not certain that they have a proper emphasis on what is "good or bad".

What is often used is the formula that currently prevails among influential thinkers in the photographic niche. This formula, or what we should call it, is not a measuring standard for anything at all. It is more about these individuals getting so many to listen to them that after a number of years it seems as if they understand what they are talking about. Don't trust them though! How should you go about knowing whether the photographs you make hold a decent standard? There are, of course, activities that partially help to resolve this issue.

However, there are no shortcuts, as is usually often said about the quest for success. Thus, there is every reason to believe that it applies to photography as well. My best advice is learning as much as possible. Get like-minded to spend time with – people who are more or less obsessed with photography. Show your photographs to them, look at their photographs and listen to what they say about their and your pictures.

You can jointly discuss what the photographs tell you and you learn, while teaching your peers. You will feel that most of them do not have a good understanding of theory and technology, but often these photographers are a bit of a "natural" – they may very well achieve "loaded" photographs, although they are not really ready to explain how they have gone about it. Depth of field blurry background, for which they have, however, learned a Japanese term and call it "bokeh" and uses it very diligently. In addition to techniques and compositions and general views, not many people think about the most important thing about a photograph – it should tell something. If photography does not, it may be ever so technically high-level and compositionally equilibristic, but the most important thing is missing and that is the story.

Use what you learn from others, whether they are friends, people you've met at photo exhibitions or courses. However, don't let any idea rule you just because someone said that is how it should be. You have to perform and experiment yourself. In the digital era, we can go out one day and make a thousand images during an afternoon to learn how to see the sun reflected against a brick wall. Well then, it's the sunlight that makes the brick show colors. Set the camera's settings, learn how to get to the shots quickly. Especially in street photography, the photo opportunity shows up quickly and disappears even faster. If you are interested in street photography, you may want to consider yourself a gunman in the Wild West, always ready to shoot. You do not have time to turn on the camera, remove the lens cap and make the picture you are imagining is heading in your direction. You have to be prepared. The street motif is as fluid as a rainstorm in the desert. It is there and is over before you have your finger on the trigger after flipping the switch.

So then there are not even “bad” images, there will be no picture at all.

Playing with the formats, street photography is a very broad concept and is about taking pictures on the run “Images à la sauvette” as Henri Cartier Bresson (1952) wrote. The English term “snapshot”, I mean, describes it all better than the widespread chatter about the “decisive moment”, which feels like a matter of course for all photographs. When it comes to street photography, it is about capturing unregistered life and perpetuating it on the memory card.

The possibilities of technology

Both the reduction of the size of cameras over the last 100 years and the more automated handling (if you wish) of digital technology affects the kind of photography that can be made, what photographs are created and what photographs gain appreciation in the circle around the photographer, especially in the photo amateur cabinet. Good photographs, regardless of technology, have been made continuously throughout the history of photography. For most of the historical period when photography was included, photography has been about attaching a negative image to paper, film or various kinds of plates and then transferring the image to a positive one on paper. When computer technology made its entry into the photographic arena with digital image files, many believed that photography, as we knew it until around 1990, underwent major changes. Not only the technology of recording the subject, but even the soul of photography is considered to have been influenced by digital technology.

Jean Baudrillard (2009:45) believes that computer generated images change our relationship to the image as such. The ultimate violence against the image is the violence in computer-generated images that emerges from nothing from numerical calculations and the computer. This also stops the representation of the image, its basic "illusion", since, in computer generation, the referent no longer exists and here there is no room for the real to "take place", but it is immediately produced as virtual reality.

Digital production deletes the analog image. It erases the reality as something that can be "imagined". The photographic act, the moment of disappearance of both motifs and objects in the same instantaneous confrontation – the shutter eliminates the world and the gaze for a moment, a syncope, a *petite mort* (small death) that triggers the mechanical appearance of the image disappears in digital, numerical processing. All of this inevitably leads to the death of the photographic image as original media, Baudrillard notes. At the same time as the analog image, the essence of photography has disappeared. The analog image still attests to a vivid presence of an object for a motif – a last postponement of the spread and digital flood wave that is in readiness for us.

The problem with reference was already almost insoluble: what about the real one? Baudrillard (2009:46) wonders. What about representation? When the reference disappears with the virtual, when it disappears into the technical planning of the image, when the situation of a real world is no longer translated into a photosensitive film (it is the same with language, which is like a sensitive film of ideas), in the end, there is no longer any possible representation. Baudrillard sees how the digital image no longer represents the physical subject in the reality we have created a photograph of. We can ask ourselves how important it really is to have that connection. Doesn't photography have the same right as art painting to explore the boundaries of what a photograph can be, what it can contain and most importantly – what it can look like? What distinguishes the analog image is that it is the place where a form of distance disappearance, a "freezing" of the world, takes place. That genuineness in the heart of the picture that Warhol talked about. In the digital image, or the computer generated, there is no negative anymore, no "time lag". Nothing dies or disappears in the digital image, notes Baudrillard (2009:49). The image is just a product of a protocol and a program, which is exacerbated by automatic dissemination from one medium to another: computer, mobile phone, TV screen, etc. – the automatic nature of the network corresponding to the automatic in the design of the image. So, should we save that absence? Should we save the void and this intensity in the center of the picture? Removing meaning brings out the essentials, namely that the image is more important than what it is talking about, just as language is more important than what it means. The worst is precisely this impossible in a world without a image – playback – a world that is always captured, filmed and photographed even before it is visible. This is a deadly danger to the "real" world, but also to the image, because when it merges with the real and delves into the real and recovers it, there is no longer any image – at least not as an exception, as an illusion, like a parallel world. In the visual flow where we are currently underwater, there is not even time to become an image. Will the thoughts we have about photography be forever colored by the "technology shock" with which the transition from analog to digital technology affects us? It is difficult to determine, as with the entire introduction of new technology, there are discussions of both threats and promise regarding the use of the new technology.

Baudrillard (2009:50-51) dreams of an image that would be an "*ecriture automatique*" (automated writing) of the world's singularity, which the iconoclasts of the famous Byzantine controversies dreamed of. They claimed that only the image in which the deity was directly present – as in Veronica's sweat cloth –was authentic, an *ecriture automatique* of the divine face without any human hand having intervened through a kind of transfer / printing in analogy with the negative in photographic film. On the other hand, they vehemently rejected all icons produced by the human hand, which to them were merely simulacra of the divine, that is, compensation. As automatic light writing that neither passes through the real nor the idea of the real, photography, through this automaticity, can be said to be the prototype of the literalness of the world, without the interference of the human hand. The world produces itself as a radical illusion, as pure trace, without simulation, without human intervention, and above all, not as truth, for if there is a sovereign product of the human mind, it is the product of truth and objective reality.

Photographic instability

The physical instability of the photograph is not about the photograph being easy to destroy or even self-destruct over time. It is mostly about how we store the digital images over time. The digital files we burned CDs and DVDs to store ten years ago should be reviewed. These plastic discs are not as invariable as they were argued to be when they were introduced. Photography has a tendency to change over time – perhaps because the outside world changes as time goes by. Here we will concentrate on the instability that emerges in the stories of the photographs. When the photograph is made, it conveys a certain story. That story changes as the years pass and the photograph eventually belongs to the past. It has a bit to do with the viewer changing over time and also what the viewer sees.

In all the respects we consider a photograph, its meaning fluctuates, partly depending on which viewer is currently studying the image, and partly the prevailing idea of what is a "good image" at any given time and place. What is "good" today need not be regarded as good tomorrow, either for the individual viewers or according to the prevailing aesthetic ideas.

The photograph seems to balance between these two indications of what is an image, or some images, which do not succeed in being ranked as being an image at all. Since I started photographing digitally in 2003, I saved all the frames made until spring 2015. This according to my thesis that a "bad image today can be an acceptable image tomorrow".

When I started deleting images, I realised that if I had been young today I would not have started deleting. The deletion would mean that I would have missed the opportunity to "discover" new assets in images at later reviews. Now I do not create any such plans for the future because I have begun to realise that my time does not last forever.

However, I feel that those deleted frames may be a mistake. What if time catches up with them and turns them into photographs I think are interesting? Or if it turns out that I want to write something about the "failed photograph"?

So, I stopped deleting and should look through some hard drives for images that can be considered unsuccessful and write something about why those images are considered “unsuccessful”.

Only to reason a bit further about the instability of photography is it time to talk about whether the viewer’s emotional state is the only thing that may shift the stability of a photograph. It may not be so, but it is one of the most important factors. So, if we make ourselves speculate about everything we hold for safe / unstable, we are on the lookout for what we never gave up on understanding in photography. Maybe all of our saved concerns about what the picture means are not as important as we at first sound like? We know for sure that it gives us the simple indications of what to avoid when thinking about how to study images. It is as if we are given a reason to share with us all that we have learned to avoid it with a shrug as it is something we can never share with anyone else.

We can regard photography as stagnant “camp fires”, that is, nodes that viewers gather around and study the stories “camp” in the picture, hypnotised by what happens in the picture, lose the foothold in the room and be drawn into a parallel universe belonging to another photographer. As “campfire”, photography is highly unstable and does not carry that far, but it reaches the mind of the viewer.

Revealing the hidden secrets of photographic images

We interpret – or, to use a term similar to what we are more used to – we read pictures and photos. The interpretation comes at a later stage, when our brain has processed what we have seen. This is where the meaning is produced, the secret, or the riddle gets its explanation. We should ask ourselves is if we really have a well thought out, reflected, strategy for our reading of a photograph? Isn't it rather that our gaze scans the surroundings in a seemingly chaotic way, which is in fact far more complicated than we imagine? Sturken & Cartwright (2001:2) note that our visual experiences do not take place during isolation, they are enriched with memories and images from many different aspects of our lives. It is likely that our interpretations, or readings, of images depend on our background, profession, education and interests, in our day-to-day form, simply. To this is added how the surroundings appear at the present time. Here there is room for many impressions that attract attention or disturbance, if you wish. However, it is not easy to read a picture of the crowded world, a good picture is complicated. It can be said to be the task of the complicated image to start our reflections.

"*A photograph is a secret about a secret. The more it tells you the less you know.*" Diane Arbus quoted by Susan Sontag (1973:86).

Is viewing photography a kind of tactile world? Maurice Merleau-Ponty (1968:133) tries to explain how our gaze "senses" the visible motifs in our world. The view encloses and tastes the visible things. As if contemplation was in a relationship of established harmony with them, as if it knew them before it knew them, moving in its own way with its sudden and commanding style. We do not consider chaos, but things – so that it can finally be decided whether it is the appearance or whether it is the things that govern. What does this love for the visible mean, this art of interrogating it according to its own desires, this inspired interpretation? We might be able to find the answer in the tactile touch where the questioner and the interviewee are closer and which, after all, is a special variant of eye contact. How come I give this level to my hands and that the direction of movement manages to make me feel the structures of the elegant and the rough? Between exploration and what exploration will teach me, between my movements and what I touch, there must be a certain principle relationship, a certain kinship, according to which they are not just, like the depletion of the amoeba, vague and ephemeral deformations in bodily space, without the onset and opening to a tactile world. We really only understand what we already understand.

Maurice Merleau-Ponty (1968:134) argues that the viewer must not be alien to the world he is viewing. As soon as we consider, it is necessary that the vision (which is indicated by the double meaning of the word) be doubled with a complementary view or another view. I myself being looked at from the outside, for example if someone else would see me. We are observers and are being watched –

a constant interaction. Maybe we can say that the picture becomes part of us, or at least of our life, while we cannot speculate if we become part of the image's life.

When someone makes a statement about whether a photograph has artistic height or not, those who take part in someone's statement expect the speaker to understand what he is saying.

The French cultural sociologist Pierre Bourdieu (1979:3-6) talks about *cultural capital* as a way of consciously being able to comment on cultural phenomena. Pierre Bourdieu views cultural capital as working in three ways. The *first* part of cultural capital is described as something the individual carries, it is "carved in the body". Cultural capital is, so to speak, inseparably united with the individual's own body, it is incorporated. In this way, this part has similarities to habitus (see below). The *second* part of cultural capital is cultural objects (books, paintings, machines), which objectify variants of cultural capital. In each case, they follow the same structures that apply to "incorporated" cultural capital. The *third* part of cultural capital is academic merit. These, like coins, are, according to Bourdieu, relatively independent of the value of their bearers. This certified and guaranteed form of cultural capital raises the question of social functions in the education system and can lead to a practical awareness of the relationship between cultural capital and the economic system. I imagine the three parts work together during an individual's life cycle.

Society is described by Pierre Bourdieu (1995) as a social space in which an individual's position shapes her habitus which makes her inclined to act in certain ways. Habitus can be explained as a system of dispositions that determines the individual's perceptions of the world and the possibilities to act. The dispositions consist of collective memories, the way of moving, social experiences and more, which has become part of the individual. The dispositions in this way constitute a kind of embodiment of the individual's social conditions. A person's habitus is founded on the habits she incorporates from participating in the life of the family and school and then acts as a resilient and often unconscious pattern of action. Habitus can be regarded as embodied capital. A human habitus is thus a product of her life history. I regard this as a way of describing the "backpack" of experiences we carry with us through life and thus they have similarities to the first part of the cultural capital Bourdieu talks about. All of this is about the knowledge of what is important and how we should behave in order to appear cultured.

Systematic reading of photographic images

Having a plan is always an advantage, at least you do not risk forgetting something. It is probably important to be systematic when reading images, in the same way that it is a clear advantage to be systematic when reading linguistic texts. Here I borrow a strategy by Anette Kuhn (2007: 284), who has written about a way to go about it:

• *Take into account the human motif of photography. Start with a simple description and then move on to the subject position. In this part of the exercise, it is good to use third person ("she", rather than "me", for example). To bring out the emotions associated with the photograph, you can visualize yourself as the subject he / she was at that moment, in the picture: this can be done with all the human motifs of photography, if there are more than one and even with animals and inanimate objects in the picture.*

- *Take into account the production context of the image. Where, when, how, by whom and why was the photograph taken?*
- *Take into account the context in which an image of this kind would have been made. What photographic techniques were used? What are the aesthetics of the picture? Does it meet certain photographic conventions?*
- *Take into account the feasibility of photography in its context. Who or what was the photograph done for? Who has it now and where is it stored? Who saw it then and who sees it now?*

According to Anette Kuhn, there are opportunities to create a clear strategy for reading photographs. If you want to connect to her method, you can do it, or choose another one. However, it seems to be smart not only to go on "gut feeling" but to be a little more systematic in the reading of photographs. When we "read" the image intuitively, it is not given that it is done according to an intellectual plan, but more by automaticity.

The perspectives in pictures interested Maurice Merleau-Ponty (1960:50). Merleau-Ponty argues that you do not even have to say that the perspectives "fool us" and that distant objects are "bigger" to the naked eye than one might assume given their projection in a drawing or in a photograph – at least not by the size they concern most distant and the closest plan. The size of the moon on the horizon cannot be measured with a number of parts of the coin I hold in my hand, there is a "size of distance", a type of quality that adheres to the moon in the same way as hot and cold to other objects.

Roland Barthes (1961:128-129) also wants to try to find out what the image expresses, how to read it and ask questions: What is the content of the photographic message? What does the photograph convey? By definition, it is the scene itself, the letter itself. Of the object in the picture there is certainly a reduction: of proportions, perspective and color. This reduction is by no means a transformation (in the mathematical sense); In order to move the real to its photography, it is not necessary to cut this real into pieces and build these pieces into essentially different characters of the object they offer us to read. Between this object and its image there is no need to have a relay, that is, a code; the picture is not reality; but is nevertheless the perfect analogy and it is precisely this analogous perfection except common sense that defines photography. In this way, the special status of the photographic image seems: it is a message without code; a proposal that must immediately reach an important consequence: the photographic message is a continuous message. Are there other messages without code? At first glance yes: it is just all analog reproductions of reality: drawings, paintings, theater. In fact, each of these messages develops in an immediate and obvious way, in addition to the analogue content (scene, object, landscape), a new message, commonly known as the style of reproduction; this is a second meaning, the meaning of which is a "treatment" of the image under the influence of the author, whose meaning, or aesthetics, ideology, refers to a certain “culture” in the society that receives the message. In summary, all these “imitative” art forms have two messages: a signified message, which is the analog itself, and a connotative message, which is how society chooses to interpret, to a certain extent, what she thinks. This duplicity of messages is evident in all reproductions that are not photographic: no drawing, however “real” it is, whose accuracy is executed in a realistic style; no filmed scene whose objectivity cannot be read as the very sign of objectivity. Again, the study of these connotative messages remains to be done (it should determine whether so-called works of art can be reduced to a system of meanings); one may assume that what is common to all these imitative arts is probably about a universal symbolism or through the rhetoric of the time, with stereotypes (plans, colors, connotative code, graphics, gestures, expressions, grouping of sub-elements). What do we put into the photographic image in the form of connotations? It seems to be a soup of memories and impressions that we think captures what the picture expresses.

What Roland Barthes described as ’Studium’ and ’Punctum’ is about what everyone can experience / see in an image and what exactly makes me find the image interesting. One of all the questions that can be asked about this idea is whether the emotions that control our emotional experience of photography are in the picture or within ourselves. Is it that all our experiences, studies and the mood of the contemplative day determine whether we can “make” a photograph? That is perhaps why the European Roland Barthes (1961:138) is able to write: “*Photographs of China give us the feeling of an impenetrable universe, if it stays with the picturesque – that is, our particular cropping of our perception of China.*" That might depend on whether we grow up in, or lived in China for a long time. The exotic, that is, what we are not used to seems far more impenetrable and mysterious / magical than the parking lot outside our own house.

Jean-Claude Nancy (2005:102) notes: I write, you read. But all of us, *nous autres* "us others" who are readers and writers of texts related to photography, or perhaps of art in general (if I try to imagine who can read this text), if we want to identify ourselves we must construct an identity where not everything is given with this simple "we". Every time someone says "we" – and who would say "we" if not someone, a single person? Who can say that if not me or you? – formulates a request for identification. For this request, he suggests traits, indexes, lines, but also that he cannot confirm their immediate and intangible positions, how I, on the contrary, confirm them. I am distinguished from the rest, just like everyone else. We place the same claim, with the stated purpose of recruitment character, a demand, a desire, a desire for distinction. We must construct our "otherness", which is different only in a tendentious way. That is why we accompany "we" with parts of its request: "we photographers", "we Frenchmen", "we in this family". Similarly, a request formulated in this way acknowledges its weakness or difficulty. The question is who are the "Frenchmen", my family "or" the photographers "... are? In each case, it is necessary to either construct one or to fall back on formal and external identification (identity card, civil registers, professional identification).

We seem to constantly construct our social reality. Reality perception in itself implies a kind of coding, says John Fiske (1990:66). The codes for photography cause special problems, since photography seems to follow nature and be composed by analog dimensions. However, the search for meaning involves identifying significant differences and thus introducing digital functions into an analogous reality. Putting sixty marks around the perimeter of a dial is a metaphor for how we impose meaning on reality. So perception of reality is a coding in itself. Perception is about making sense of data in front of us: identifying important differences and thus identifying entities – perceiving what we are experiencing. When it comes to the view of the relationships between these entities, we can see them as a whole. In other words, it is about creating paradigm and syntagm. Our perception and understanding of reality is as specific as our culture is for our spoken and written languages. It is in this sense that we can speak of reality as a social construct.

The French philosopher Jean-Luc Nancy (2005:104) is interested in the non-coincidence that passes through photography. Of course, it can also work in painting. But painting has never imagined the "snapshot", where an "I" with one click coincides with an "you", another "I". The image is prepared around the usual influence, on silver film or in digital form, of the light and the eye, a view from the outside and a view from the inside, about this particular view (active) and this other one (passive). This effect is usually instantaneously split between the brilliant (photo) and its track (graphic). In its tracks it changes. Light returns to the eye (into the eye) and what it means is that it is no longer a "view" or "vision", either objective or subjective. It is, rather, the stigma of surprise that the one who "makes" the photograph and the one who "takes" in the picture are related. At that point in this stigma (photography itself), both are taken by each other by surprise and the discovery of each other. They are there, intimate and intrusive, strange and familiar to each other at the same time, as the same image. This monotony is permeated with a variant of its two consecutive subjects. According to Jean-Luc Nancy, photography is a monster with two subjects, with a double body (human) and a single, hollow head whose single eye flashes on and off.

What happens when considering an image is that we probably do not only see the current image in our reception of it. The French psychoanalyst Jacques Lacan (1961:159) points out how, by looking at images, we are reminded of other images, which are of course interpreted into the interpretation of the image we consider. The characters that are photographed, so ironically in the film, with a small apparatus, are sometimes irresistibly reminiscent of the group, also photographed countless times. Does this mean that they are still affected? No more than the apostles. It is precisely at this level that they could bear the best testimony. It is because of a certain naivety, a certain poverty, a certain innocence that most have instructed us best. It is true that those around Socrates were more brilliant and that they teach us no less about the transfer. Maybe this is the key point, in all education we become more receptive to a message, a meaning, when we imagined that we should find it, in a picture?

Jean-Luc Nancy (2005:106) argues that in a photograph

there is always something hallucinatory, something that has lost its way or is not in its place. While painting – or filmmaking – manages to present in a completely different way, bringing us in close proximity with a variant of presence, the photograph, which at first seems inclined to work in the same direction, is transferred to an indelible removal of its own presence. It is lost as soon as it has been copied – which is, however, deducted from nothing – it is revoked from our grasp ability, hidden and secret. Even the worst photograph openly reveals a secret, and that is done by transforming everything into an "otherness" the more it changes by being close to us, in that it refers us to our familiar immediacy. Consequently, it always mutters *a nous autres* : us (others) who are exposed, who are enlightened by the sun, moon and projectors, we (others) who are the strange beings in this world of day and night, we (others) who surprise us by to see ourselves, to turn to visions, by photosynthesising ourselves, we humans and shadows of people, we are our most real and thus our strangest, most alien others.

The secret of photography, Jean-Luc Nancy (2006:106) says, is the very clear mystery of being lost and wandering, its escape into the strange middle of the familiar. The photo captures the familiar and the immediate and transforms itself into alienation. By capturing its own trade-offs, it leads to what it catches on the trade-offs. The photograph disturbs, it disturbs us. Between the motive for clicks and the captured motive, there is a coexistence without coincidence, or there is a coincidence without contact, or a contact without connection (which is the law of contact). The meeting is ineffective in its effectiveness (which is about the law of the meeting). In this way we can see the surface of the photograph in the same seemingly inexplicable way that Roland Barthes's (1993:25ff) "Punctum" draws our attention somewhat. "Punctum" stands for a disturbance, or a beat mark in "Studium". "Punctum" stands for the content of what stands out from the picture.

Maurice Merleau-Ponty (1960:256) points to the irony of how the afterlife uses people's lives. Trotsky's grave, if one is to believe the newspaper photographs, wears a hammer and sickle, nothing distinguishes this emblem from the Soviet Union. So Trotsky, after his death, continues to assert solidarity with the October Revolution. But it is Trotsky's fate, it is the conclusion of Trotsky's life. Trotsky, who is still living in what he wrote, suggests a question that the stone from the tomb does not answer. It would be our joint responsibility to respond. It makes me think of the movie about the musician Björn Afzelius, who has written many good songs, got its title from a song written by the Danish singer Anne Linnet (Tusind Stykker), or "Thousand Bits" for which Björn Afzelius had written the Swedish lyrics. The irony of that!

Capital undoubtedly also produces a banalizing generalisation of the body and of the neighbor, states Jean-Luc Nancy (2008:91). Photographic obsessions with audiences attest to this fact, with their misery, their panic, with numbers as such or with erotic obsessions filtering through everything. Most miserable is the proximity to the banal reproduction of the supposedly "singular" of the body – through millions of copies. (This is also why the "body" has also become the faddest, the flattest, the most "disconnected" of themes and terms – in irreversible coma.) But we have to take a careful look. The fear of banality, of reproduction, of celebrating the unique, the exceptional, is the banality given in a world that is currently crumbling under our feet. We are all banally doubtful of "banality" – and of this overload of banality that we attach to the body. But do we know what "banal" is?

The French phenomenological philosopher Maurice Merleau-Ponty (2005:360-362) argues that reflections and light are often poorly reproduced in photography because they are transformed into objects and, for example, in a movie, a person entering a cellar holds a lamp, we do not see the ray of light as an intangible entity exploring darkness and picking out objects, as it solidifies and can no longer show us the object at its distant end. Light moving across a wall only produces pools of dazzling brightness that are located not on the wall, but on the surface of the film. Lighting and reflection then play their role only if they remain in the background as discrete intermediaries and guide our gaze instead of stopping it. But what should we understand? When I am led through a strange apartment towards its proprietors, there is someone who knows on my behalf, for whom the development of the visual spectacle has a meaning and who moves towards a goal and I lend myself to this knowledge that I do not have. When any detail of a landscape that I have not been able to discern alone is pointed out to me, it is someone who has already seen it, who already knows where you stand and where to look to see it. The lighting controls my gaze and makes me see the object, so that in a way it knows about and sees the object. If I imagine a theater without an audience where the curtain goes up over illuminated landscapes, I get the impression that the spectacle is visible or ready to be seen and that the light that explores the foundation and foreground lifts the shadows and permeates the stage throughout, in a way that is as perplexing as our vision. Conversely, our own vision only takes up its own account and carries through the scope of the scene through these paths traced to it by illumination, just as when we hear a meaning, we are surprised to discover traces of a foreign thought.

We perceive in accordance with the light, as we do with other people in verbal communication. Just as communication presupposes a certain amount of linguistic environment through which a meaning is present in words, so perception requires in us an apparatus that can respond to the urges of light in accordance with its feeling (that is, in accordance with both its orientation and its meaning, which amounts to one thing), concentrate on the diffuse acidity and complete what was only foreshadowed in the play. This apparatus is the gaze, in other words, the natural connection between appearances and our kinesthetic propagation, something that is not experienced as a law, but is experienced as the involvement of our body in the typical structures of a world. Lighting and the permanence of the illuminated things, which are correlated with it, are directly dependent on our physical situation.

Does the surface of the image make sense? Czech-born Brazilian philosopher Villém Flüsser (2000:8) thinks that when we look at pictures, we scan them and take in their inherent meaning. Pictures are surfaces with meaning. Images – foremost – mean something “out there” in time and space that they must make understandable to us as abstractions (such as limitations of the four dimensions of time and space to length and breadth). This specific ability to abstract surfaces of time and space and project them back into space and time is what is called "imagination". It is a prerequisite for production and deciphering of images. In other words: the ability to encode phenomena in two-dimensional symbols and read these symbols. Flüsser considers the importance of the images on the surface. You can take them in with a single glance, but it remains superficial. If one wants to deepen the meaning, that is, to reconstruct abstracted dimensions, one must allow the gaze to wander across the surface and feel the way when doing so. This walk across the surface of the image is called "scanning". Then a glance follows a complex path formed on the one hand by the structure of the image and on the other by the intentions of the observer. The meaning of the image revealed in the process of scanning therefore constitutes a synthesis of two intentions: one manifest in the image and the other belongs to the viewer. It follows that the images are not "denotative" (unambiguous) complexes of symbols (such as numbers, for example), but "connotative" (ambiguous) complexes of symbols: They provide room for interpretation. We often find different sentences in an image, because we are different individuals.

Magic and traces

Villém Flüsser (2000: 9) argues that space and time that are characteristic of the image are nothing but the world of magic, a world where everything is repeated and where everything participates in a significant context. Such a world is structurally different from the linear world of history where nothing is repeated and where everything has causes and will have consequences. In the historical world, for example, the sunrise is the reason why the rooster goes crazy; in the magical world, sunrise means rejoicing and madness means sunrise. The meaning of images is magical.

Flüsser's thoughts on images as magical are on the way to considering photographic images that Susan Sontag (1973:120) expressed. Sontag's idea is that photographs should be considered as tracks. American writer and filmmaker Susan Sontag argues that a photograph is not just an image (in the way a painting is an image), an interpretation of the real; it is also a trace, something that is directly imprinted by the real, like a footprint or a death mask. Perhaps this is one of the reasons why we enjoy looking so much at older photographs, especially where nostalgic emotions fill us as we look at them.

The photographic image and the subconscious

The things we know that a photograph should contain are not with certainty the ones it will contain. If we imagine those photographs in a way we should have done with all the photographs we have ever taken. That is, as something that is partly a capture of reality, a fraction of a second, but also as a voice from our own subconscious, something we are not really aware of.

Is photography a kind of Ikea edition of psychoanalysis? Sigmund Freud (2005:139) made the comparison between the negative of photography and its positive copy when he spoke of the subconscious. The negative then represents the subconscious, which is then copied and whose positive copy enters the conscious world. The conscious grabs something out of the subconscious and presents it to the general public.

Maybe it is hard to take in, but there is something soul-cleansing, with elements of increased self-insight, in looking at oneself with the help of the photographs we have made. The surprise we can experience over older pictures we have taken probably has to do with the time that has elapsed and that we have gained a lot of impressions since we took the picture, partly through the things we hopefully learned since taking the photograph we now look at with relatively new eyes.

These are the "new" eyes we use to learn more about what we already know, but need help to see what it is. Where we learn to see the compositions we make as a result of a voice from within. If we make many "desolate" photographs, which among other things I love to do, what does that mean? Am I empty inside and like when it is reflected in the photographs I make? Or is my interior so full of rumbling thoughts that I "rest" by photographing the most desolate places I see around me? Whatever is the answer to this, I become convinced that there is a link down in the subconscious, a link that is not so obvious. Of course, it is possible that we make a lot of photographs that are "copies" of photographs that others have created. It probably happens because we want to see if we can achieve a similar expression.

The difficulties with this is that we do not fill the photographs with the stories that are unique to us. Then it becomes difficult to see any sense in making photographs that point too closely to photographs others have made before us. At the same time, there may not be so many alternative paths to choose. In other forms of expression such as literature, painting, music and film, many articles are deeply "influenced" by other, former authors.

We remember the Japanese terms "sensei" and "gakusei" which are usually translated with "teacher" and "pupil", or as "the one who precedes" and "the one who follows". We can assume that we all follow a "sensei", but the question is whether there is a point when we are on our own playing field, are we in our own laboratory? Or, will there always be traces of other people's work in what we create?

A comparison can be the spoken language. I speak Swedish, mainly like my mother did, growing up in Stockholm and because I also grew up there. I had a father who was from Skåne (in the south) where we went on vacation almost every summer, I did my military service in Umeå (in the north), visiting relatives in Västerbotten's outbacks which was grandmother's home area. I have worked in Ystad (in the south) and Gothenburg (on the west coast). I have acquired expressions such as *hialös*, *lemmalytt*, *anvar*, *bamba* and *svale*. The dialectal vocabulary is mostly passive, I cannot speak a dialect that would make the natives believe that I come from Västerbotten, Skåne or the West Coast. However, I understand them well. However, I continue, for the most part, to speak a kind of middle-class stockholmian idiom, which is a product of the school system, but also of the influences from Gothenburg where I could be threatened with a blow to the head when speaking a distinctly stockholmian dialect, so I slightly dampened the childhood dialect.

Similarly, I mean that it is about photography – we admire the work of some photographers – we wish we could make pictures similar to the ones they make. When we try to think of it, the remnants of these admired images remain in our subconscious and act as a rulers or guides. These desires are incorporated into what kind of photographer we want to be. To this is added the luggage we have, what Pierre Bourdieu (1979:3-6) calls "habitus", the backpack of cultural conceptions and knowledge we carry with us through life. This creates possible directions for what kind of photographs we consider to be good images of the ones we create. In this way you may state that it is not we who "decide" what is good, we only have a feeling that a picture is good, but it is only when the viewer comes into the game that we get other people's reactions to our pictures. The viewer refills from their own luggage and makes their interpretation of what your image is on a scale. However, it is your images, you should not care too much about what others say about them.

If the pictures appear good to you, then you feel that you know your subconscious and the images are thus a part of you.

Our relationship with photography

What does a common relationship with photography look like for people – if there is one? In a way, can say that we take photography for granted, it's something we've always had a relationship with, which can make us underestimate its importance. The question is whether the photograph does not deserve better. Should photography not be taken more seriously and considered as a way for us to use our experience to meet the deluge of stimuli that a photograph entails for us viewers to create further strong stories?

We can express our views as: “this is a nasty photograph of me”. Then we probably mean that the image in question does not capture us like the inner image we have made of ourselves. That points to is that the person who just made that “ugly” photograph is in a different story and not necessarily a story that overlaps with the story we ourselves think we participate in, belonging in our own lives and the representations of ourselves as individuals in the image. We find it difficult to get this story to match how we think the different stories are connected.

When we are influenced by a picture, it is, as noted earlier, reflections of one’s self, we read things into the story that we let participate in the game about our lives. In the past, people carried pictures with their loved ones in the wallet – today these photographs are in the cell phone. There they do not get the nicely worn patina that the wallet photographs received. In this way, the analog time had its absolute charm. It is also the way my generation has become accustomed to. We think, even if we try to be “up to date”, that it is the original way to carry the stories of our lives with us.

One question that may be put is whether our relationship with photography is a relationship in the same sense as those we have with people or whether it is a completely different relationship. The photograph can be regarded as an object, a thing and we have been given space for the stories we want them to include. Objectively speaking, photography does not have its own stories or memories to influence the surroundings. Still, that's exactly what some photographs do.

In all the units or parts that a photograph is made of, it can be said that it has width and height. In terms of depth, there is only insofar as any kind of perspective works in photography. A kind of technical depth that we probably should not be so positive about. Once we have learned to make up the world of photography from constructed perspectives, it is a matter between the author and the viewer that we translate into perspective theory.

As far as photography is concerned, it is a deeply hidden insight into what we should let photography allow this to see the light of day. As if it's part of everything we consciously try to avoid getting ourselves into. Those relationships are far too difficult to sort out, but we should really be happy to make our attempts. Is it that the relationship to the photograph is really about our relationship to the story of the photograph?

It seems that we can participate in as many stories as possible and still consider those stories as parts of one and the same story. After starting to study photographs, a period occurs when we all become "image addicts" and absorb huge amounts of information by studying a great many images during that period.

The stories of the photographs catch us and create a craving, the more pictures we view, the more we want to share. It is as if we are looking for the resolution of the stories, the end of the story or something similar. Even though we have discovered something that reminds us of this end, we still do not stop looking at pictures. The images we see we chase into the ongoing story so that the parts of the stories we see in photographs become difficult to distinguish from the parts we encounter in other parts of our lives.

It is as if the stories of photography tell us their course of action that borders our lives and we never want to stop maximising the stories. This seems to be very similar to a drug addiction. It is suddenly very difficult to stop because we have integrated image viewing into our lives. The only "cure" seems to be to continue the vain search for a story thread that ties together all the rumbling stories. We don't know for sure why all those story threads flutter in the wind, grab our attention and seduce us.

The aesthetics of photography

What is aesthetics in terms of art and specifically - what is the aesthetics of photography? Aesthetics is, generally speaking, from an individual perspective an attempt to describe the human reaction to beauty and art. This is based on defining these words and clarifying their relationship to each other. Aesthetics are also believed to explain how man perceives and perceives art. Aesthetics is also about deciding whether concepts such as "beauty" have primarily subjective meaning and explain what happens in a psychological aspect when a person "consumes" a work of art.

Key issues in aesthetics are the relationship of art to the beautiful and the sublime, the relationship between fiction and reality, as well as the question of the cultural and social function of art. Other central issues are whether art may be objectively evaluated, to determine whether the author's intention or the objective interpretation has more validity than the other's, and to assess the art's expression, originality, individuality and context. As can be seen from this rather general definition of aesthetics, it is very much about assessment, how high level of objectivity aesthetics expresses and whose validation is to be used.

To link to the aesthetics of photography, we go to a text by Susan Sontag where she describes her view on the aesthetics of photography. A few days after her death in December 2014, we could read it in the newspaper Dagens Nyheter. The pivotal point in Sontag's view of the aesthetics of photography is that the modern view is fragmentary:

"*We perceive reality as essentially infinite and knowledge as unlimited. It follows that all boundaries and all unifying ideas must be deceptive, demagogic; at best provisional; almost always, in the long run, untrue. To view reality based on certain unifying ideas has the advantage that it gives shape to our experiences. But – and this is what we learn from the modern vision – it simultaneously denies the infinite diversity and complexity of real life. In this way, it stifles our operation, yes, even our right to recreate what we want to recreate – our society, ourselves. What is liberating, we are told, is that we can perceive more and more.* " (Susan Sontag, 2014)

Sontag also points out that photography is a way of seeing, but that it is not the human view as such. At its height, it is part of human vision or contemplation. It is also, one might think, part of the vision that has achieved almost ironic status. Sontag even believes that we can never complete photography because not only the modern look, but also the photography to its "nature" is fragmentary. In a way, our lives are merely fragmentary because, for the vast majority of us, they are made up of about 30,000 days of fragmentary "now", which are added to one another, overlapping, but not completely. We live in a constantly repeated "now", where we have the opportunity to make photographs all the time. Whether we do it or not, our "now" is there, if we do not make photographs, these "now's" may be lost as memories. Or they are made into photographs by other authors who happen to photograph us.

Thanks to the photograph, mankind has been given the power to look at its surroundings with new eyes, noted the German-French photographer and photo historian Gisèle Freund (1980:198) in her dissertation as early as in the 1930s. The value of a photographic image cannot be measured purely from an aesthetic point of view, argues Freund. The photograph must also be judged by the human and social intensity of its visual representation.

Photography is not just a way of discovering reality, as nature viewed through the camera differs from nature seen by the human eye.

The camera affects our way of seeing and creates a "new vision". Thus, with the help of the camera, we have been offered new perspectives on the world in which we live.

André Bazin (1967:15-16) argues that aesthetic qualities in photography should be sought in its power to expose reality. It is not the job of the individual to distinguish in the complex web of the objective world a reflection on a damp pavement or a child's gesture. Only the emotionless lens peels objects from all these ways of seeing stacked preconceived meanings, the spiritual dust and dirt that my eyes have covered it with and can present it in all its virgin purity for my attention and thus; for my love. Through the power of photography, the natural image of a world we neither know nor can see, nature finally does more than imitate art: it imitates the artist.

This is, according to Bazin, a lot about WHO makes the picture we then consider. Bazin argues that photography can surpass the more traditional art of creative power. The painter's aesthetic world is of a different kind from the world around him. Its boundaries encompass a significantly and substantially different microcosm. The photographic image as such and the object itself do share a common existence, like a fingerprint, which is removed from the finger of which it is an imprint. Therefore, says Bazin, photography can actually contribute something to the order of natural creation instead of providing a substitute for it. Surrealists fathomed this when they realised that the photographic plate could provide them with their marvels and for this reason: the surrealist does not care that his aesthetic purpose and the mechanical effect of the image on our imagination are different things. For the surrealist, the logical difference between what is thought and what is really disappearing tends to disappear. Each image should be viewed as an object and each object as an image. The photographic image is therefore ranked highly in surrealist creativity as it provides an image that is a reality in nature, namely a hallucination which is also a fact. The fact that surrealist paintings combine tricks and visual deception with a meticulous attention to detail reinforces this.

Gilles Deleuze (2003:87) has opinions on the flow of photographs around us in today's society. We are besieged by photographs that are illustrations, by magazines that are stories, by cinema pictures and by TV pictures. Compared to people who lived in the 19th century, the number of man-made images and photographs that we see during our lives has increased enormously. A settler in the Västerbotten hinterland in the late 19th century did not see in no way as many photographs during his / her life compared to what we are exposed to during a normal day on the Internet.

Pierre Bourdieu (1990:78) mentions the multiplication that gives rise to some of the contradictions in the approach to mechanical reproduction, which, by abolishing effort, risks depriving the work of the value it seeks to give since it meets the criteria of the complete work of art. A contradiction that is all the more sharp since the artwork, especially when it is not open, always provokes the fear of being deceived; the healthiest guarantee against this is the artist's sincerity, a sincerity that is measured by the artist's efforts and sacrifices. The unclear situation of photography in the system of fine arts may, among other things, lead to this contradiction between the value of the work, which realises the aesthetic ideal that is still most widespread and the value of the act that produces it. The "minimal" work involved in the creation of a photograph itself has made it difficult for photographers to create a place in the art world. Bourdieu thinks that this need not only be attributed to the art world. If I hire a craftsman then the value of her work is not just the time, say 45 minutes, which she needs to address the problem she was called there on the spot. I pay her, above all, for me to take advantage of the fact that she knows what to do and that she has the tools required for it. The artist, on her part, can be said to get paid (possibly) because she knows how to make a work of art.

Carl Gelderloos (2014:553) argues that photography is not as simple as taking away the photographed object from its historical context and thus hiding this context; Walter Benjamin has the additional function of repackaging the existing reality ("the world as it is") with modern luster, turning the photographed object into an object for the consumer's enjoyment. What exists is sold, with the help of photography, as something new. Of course, this is the logic of advertising and Benjamin linked photography, fashion and advertising. Although we separate the issue of advertising and the final judgments of consumer culture that may accompany it, it is clear that for Benjamin and Brecht, the photographic surface obscures an underlying reality rather than providing access to it.

The photo outside of time

Without exaggeration, we can conclude that the majority of photographs made without assignments, that is, in principle as a hobby, will never survive the year they were made. This may be because they are not sufficiently time marked with clothing, equipment, back-drops or other time markers that fork into the photograph of the epoch the image is made. These belong to a first group.

The second group of photographs are deliberately made

without time markers (often with a little more ambition). These have the ability to show up at all times with comments like, "Look, how small a human being is!" Here are these photographs, which by their scaled-down appearance become "timeless" in a positive sense.

This raises a number of questions. For me, a difficult-to-interpret image is more rewarding than a "simple" image. What do I see, what do I think I see in this picture (Bornholm, Denmark, 1962)? This is a photograph of me and my mother in 1962 in Dueodde on Bornholm. I know the geographical location because my mother is 42 years old and I am 15. I remember the "moment". When I now look at the photograph, I realise that at the age of 15 I was taller than my mother. This is what I think photography represents. Of course, for any other viewer, it does not have these connotations – the picture may seem rather unattractive – a young man and a middle-aged woman striding along some sand dunes. Another viewer would probably give this photograph low ratings on a scale of meaning.

When I look at that image we will always be staying at our age, with that look. Our clothing puts us in the 1960s, but since the image has been preserved for over 50 years, the image acts like a time machine for me, perhaps to a lesser extent for some other viewer. On the one hand, the story is out of time since it can travel through time, and perhaps the photograph simply tells about another time? At least it is not excluded.

As time passes, this photograph is still the same, but it changes as the viewer (me) gets older and develops a different relationship to the image, and time. The story is in a sense the same, but there is a gradual shift in it as I get older. Although the picture is the same, its psychological contribution in the story shows that I have grown older. The French semiotician Roland Barthes (1993:96) argues about the opposite relationship between life and death in historical images. In every photograph depicting a person, death is always present, Barthes says.

Do we learn what it takes to understand a photograph in the past, present or future? Maybe all photographs do not really account for the time they are made in, but our perception that the "real" time is a different one? Then, now and then, is a practical division of time for the organisation of human society, but in terms of photographs there is really only the present, the time when the image was created. What complicates it all is that the photograph will soon represent one then in one since we have already stepped into it.

We can see that the image is "old", from the past, and / or from the last century. It does not fit into our present day other than as a representative of the "old", the past. We can't really place all those references in the image, all the stories that started. The result is that we become disoriented without the opportunity for the story of photography to confront us as viewers.

The photograph stands as soon as it is exposed next to the general time axis we use to mark then, now and for a long time. Of course, this is the natural way of doing things. Where is the time in photography? Is it our retina that is the boundary, or is there something in the story we see that we can take on and live off of all that is made better by the fact that time stands still, balloons, or falls for its own story? Can't the story stay on track anymore, but is an entity alongside the story without what we learn from photography?

We live in the time we are surrounded by, but also all the times that existed before our existence and the times to come. Time is an abstraction in the same way that photography abstracts our world as we press the shutter button. The seriousness of this is that the photograph seems to be out of time in a way. How can a photograph then "determine the time"?

The question is whether the time and the embalming, determine time, or whether this is merely a document among all others to be interpreted and reinterpreted. The embalming perhaps the viewer is responsible for when studying photography?

Time, as a concept, never stands still, it is a machine, a clock that ticks. It is only in photographs that we may argue that time has stopped – although it can also be questioned whether the time axis has "stopped" at the same point for all viewers. The photograph is part of everything that existed at that time when the photograph was created.

So, does that mean it's a time we talk about when we say that photography embalms time? It is probably not so that all the time, say one year, in the 50s could be cramped into a solitary photograph.

We think that a photograph is "time-specific" – that is, tells a lot about a certain period. Actually, the photograph of my mother and me just says something about that moment on the way home from the beach in 1962. With my mother in the sand. A long time ago.

Literature

Adams, Anselm. 1981. *The negative.* New York & Boston. Little, Brown and Company.

Adorno, Theodor W. 1991. (1972-76) *The culture industry: selected essays on mass culture*. London: Routledge.

Barthes, Roland. 1961. Le message photographique. I: *Communications,* 1, 1961. pp. 127-138.

Barthes, Roland. 1993. (1980) *Camera Lucida: reflections onphotography.* New ed. London: Vintage.

Baudrillard, Jean. 1983. *Simulations*. Semiotext*[e].*

Baudrillard, Jean. 2001. *Seduction.* Montreal: New World Perspectives CultureTexts Series.

Baudrillard, Jean. 2002 (2000). *Screened Out.* London, New York: VERSO.

Baudrillard, Jean. 2009 (2007). *Why Hasn't Everything Already Disappeared?* London, New York, Calcutta: Seagull Books.

Bazin, André. 1960. The Ontology of the Photographic Image. I: *Film Quarterly*, Vol. 13, No. 4. (Summer, 1960), pp. 4-9.

Bazin, André. 1967. *What is cinema? Essays selected and translated by Hugh Gray*. Berkeley, Los Angeles and London: University of California Press.

Benjamin, Walter. 1974. (1935-1939). *Das Kunstwerk im Zeitalter seiner technischen Reproduzierbarkeit.* Suhrkamp.

Benjamin, Walter. 1983. *Charles Baudelaire: A Lyric Poet in the Era of High Capitalism.* London: Verso.

Benjamin, Walter. 2008. (1936) *The Work of Art in the Age of Its Technological Reproducibility, and Other Writings on Media.* Cambridge: Massachusetts, London: England. The Belknap Press of Harvard University Press.

Berger, John. 1972. *Ways of Seeing.* London: British Broadcasting Corporation and Penguin Books.

Bergström, Bo. 2000. *Bild & Budskap: ett triangeldrama om bildkommunikation.* Stockholm: Carlssons.

Bollon, Patrice. 2002. *Esprit d'Époque - Essai sur l'âme contemporaine et le conformisme naturel de nos sociétes.* Paris: Seuil.

Boulanger, Chantale. 1996. L'irréel photographique. I: *Applied Semiotics/Sémiotique appliquée* 1:2 (1996), 159-172.

Bourdieu, Pierre. 1990. (1965) *Photography: a middle-brow art.* Cambridge: Polity in association with Blackwell.

Bourdieu, Pierre. 1979. Les trois états du capital culturel. I: *Actes de la recherche en sciences* sociales. Vol. 30, novembre 1979. pp. 3-6.

Bourdieu, Pierre. 1992 (1990). *The logic of practice.* Polity Press.

Bourdieu, Pierre. 1995. (1990) *Praktiskt förnuft. Bidrag till en handlingsteori.* Göteborg: Bokförlaget *Daidalos AB.*

Bremmer, Magnus. 2015. *Konsten att tämja en bild : Fotografiet och läsarens uppmärksamhet i 1800-talets Sverige.* Diss. Lund: Mediehistoria, Lunds universitet. Mediehistoriskt arkiv 29.

Brown, Elspeth H. & Phu, Thy. (red) 2014. *Feeling photography.* Durham and London: Duke University Press.

Burgin, Victor. 1980. *The End of Art Theory: Criticism and Postmodernity.* Macmillan.

Burgin, Victor (ed.). 1982. *Thinking Photography.* London: Macmillan Press Ltd.

Burroughs, William. 1963. The Cut Up Method. I: Leroi Jones, ed., *The Moderns: An Anthology of New Writing in America* New York: Corinth Books.

Broady, Donald. 1998. *Kapitalbegreppet som utbildningssociologiskt verktyg.* Skeptronhäften / Skeptron Occasional Papers nr 1, 1998.

Boulanger, Chantale. 1996. L'irréel photographique. I: *Applied Semiotics/Sémiotique appliquée* 1:2 (1996), 159-172.

Camus, Albert. 1955 (1942). *The Myth Of Sisyphus And Other Essays.* New York: Knopf.

Cartier-Bresson, Henri. 1952. *The Decisive Moment.* New York, Simon and Schuster.

Centre National de la Photographie. 1983. *W. Eugene Smith.* Paris: Centre National de la Photographie.

de Certeau, Michel. 1984.(1980) *The Practice of Everyday Life.* Berkely, Los Angeles, London: University of California Press.

Confino, Alon. 2008. Memory and the History of Mentalities. I: Erll, Astrid & Nünning, Ansgar (eds). 2008. *Cultural Memory Studies: An International and Interdisciplinary Handbook.* Berlin · New York: Walter de Gruyter.

Cosman, Teodora. 2012.The Metaphors of Photography and the Metaphors of Memory: Artistic Reflections on an Album of Family Photographs, I: *Philobiblon* Vol. XVII (2012) No. 1.

Crary, Jonathan. 1988. Modernizing Vision. I: *Vision and Visuality.* Hal Foster (ed) 1988. Seattle: Bay Press.

Crary, Jonathan. 1990. T*echniques of the observer, on vision and modernity in the nineteenth century.* Cambridge, Massachusetts; London, England: MIT Press.

De Haene Rosique, María Margarita. 2009. *París y la fotografía, pasión de luz: Mirada fotográfica y visión moderna.* Universidad Autónoma de Querétaro, Serie Bellas Artes, México.

Deleuze, Gilles. 1986. (1983) *Cinema 1: The Movement-Image*, Minneapolis: University of Minnesota Press.

Deleuze, Gilles. 2003. (1981) *Francis Bacon: The Logic of Sensation.* London, New York: Continuum.

Derrida, Jacques. 2010. *Copy, Archive, Signature: A Conversation on Photography. Edited with an Introduction by Gerhard Richter.* Stanford University Press, Stanford, California.

Dewey, John. 1980 (1934). *Art as Experience.* New York: Perigee Books.

Ducasse, C. J. 1964. Art and the Language of the Emotions. I: *The Journal of Aesthetics and Art Criticism*, Vol. 23, No. 1, In Honor of Thomas Munro. (Autumn, 1964), pp. 109-112.

Dusl, Andrea Maria. 2014. *Aufnahme und Auswahl: Strategien fotografischer Praxis.* Diss. Wien: Universität für angewandte Kunst Wien.

Eco, Umberto 1982. Critique of the Image. I: Burgin, Victor (ed.). *Thinking Photography.* London: Macmillan Press Ltd.

Ekström, Anders, Jülich, Solveig & Snickars, Pelle (red). 2006. *1897: Mediehistorier kring Stockholmsutställningen.* Statens ljud- och bildarkiv.

Fiske, John. 1990. (1982) *Introduction to Communication Studies.* London, New York: Routledge.

Flusser, Vilém. 2000. (1983) *Towards a Philosophy of Photography.* London: Reaktion Books.

Freund, Gisèle. 1980 (1974) *Photography & Society.* Boston: David. Godine. Publisher, Inc.

Freud, Sigmund. 2005. (1986) *The Essentials Of Psycho-Analysis.* Selection by Anna Freud. London, Vintage Books.

Gelderloos, Carl. 2014. Simply Reproducing Reality—Brecht, Benjamin, and Renger-Patzsch on Photography. I: *German Studies Review* 37.3 (2014): 549–573.

Gibian, Peter., 2011. The Image and its Discontents: Hawthorne, Poe, and the Double Bind of 'Iconoclash', I: *Journal of the Short Story in English* [Online], 56 | Spring 2011, Online since 01 June 2013, connection on 19 March 2015. URL : http://jsse.revues.org/1138

Gitelman, Lisa & Pingree, Geoffrey B. (eds.) 2004. *New Media, 1740-1915*. MIT press.

Gitelman, Lisa. 2006. *Always Already New: Media, History, and the Data of Culture*. London, Cambridge: The MIT Press.

Haggerty, Kevin D. & V. Ericson, Richard. 2000. The surveillant assemblage. I: *British Journal of Sociology* Vol. No. 51 Issue No. 4 (December 2000) pp. 605–622.

Hall, Edward T. 1990 (1966). *The Hidden Dimension.* Toronto, New York: The Anchor Books.

Higgins, Jackie. 2013. *Why It Does Not Have To Be In Focus: Modern Photography Explained*, New York, Thames & Hudson.

Hossaini, Ali. 2003. Vision of the Gods:An Inquiry Into the Meaning of Photography. I: *Logos* 2.3 – Summer 2003.

Ekström, Anders, Jülich, Solveig & Snickars, Pelle (red). 2006. *1897: Mediehistorier kring Stockholmsutställningen.* Statens ljud- och bildarkiv.

Kember, Sarah J. 2008. The Virtual Life of Photography. I: *Photographies* Vol. 1, No. 2, September 2008, pp. 175–203.

Krauss, Rosalind. 1978. Tracing Nadar. I: *October*, Vol. 5, Photography. (Summer, 1978), pp. 29-47.

Kuhn, Anette. 2007. Photography and cultural memory: a methodological exploration. I: *Visual Studies*, Vol. 22, No. 3, December 2007.

Lacan, Jacques. 1981. (1973) *The seminar of Jacques Lacan. Book XI, The four fundamentals of Psychoanalysis.* New York, London: W.W.Norton & Company.

Lacroix, Michel. 2001. *Le culte de l'émotion.* Paris: Flammarion.

Latour, Bruno. 1993. (1991) *We Have Never Been Modern.* Cambridge, Massachusetts: Harvard University Press.

Latour, Bruno & Hermant, Emilie. 1998. *Paris ville invisible.* Paris: La Découverte-Les Empêcheurs de penser en rond.

Lefebvre, Henri. 1991. (1947) *Critique of Everyday Life: Volume I.* Verso, London & New York.

Lyotard, Jean-François. 1984. (1979) *The postmodern condition: a report on knowledge*. Manchester: Manchester Univ. Press.

McLuhan, Marshall. 1967. (1964) *Media: Människans utbyggnader.* Stockholm: Bokförlaget PAN/Norstedts.

Merleau-Ponty, Maurice. 1960. *Signes*. Paris: Les Éditions Gallimard.

Merleau-Ponty, Maurice. 1968 (1964). *The Visible and the Invisible.* Evanston: Northwestern University Press.

Merleau-Ponty, Maurice. 2005. (1945) *Phenomenology of Perception.* London and New York: Routledge.

Mitchell, William J. 1992. *The reconfigured eye: visual truth in the post-photographic era*. Cambridge, Mass.: MIT Press.

Mitchell, William J. T. 1994. *Picture Theory: essays on verbal and visual representation.* London: University of Chicago Press.

Mitchell, W. J. T. 1996. What Do Pictures "Really" Want? I: *October*, Vol. 77. (Summer, 1996), pp. 71-82.

Mitchell, W. J. T. 2005. *What do pictures want?: the lives and loves of images*. Chicago: University of Chicago Press.

Molderings, Herbert. 2014. Photographic History in the Spirit of Constructivism: Reflections on Walter Benjamin's "Little History of Photography". In: Art in Translation, Volume 6, Issue 3, pp. 317-344.

Nancy, Jean-Luc. 2005. (1999) *The ground of the image. New York: Fordham University Press.*

Nancy, Jean-Luc. 2008. (2006) *Corpus*. New York: Fordham University Press.

Panayotopoulos, Nikos. 2008. *Terra Cognita: The Western Hegemonic Representations Of Greece Through the Case of Athens*. Student thesis. University of Derby, Great Britain.

Parsons, Sarah. 2009. Sontag's Lament: Emotion, Ethics, and Photography. I: *Photography & Culture*, Volume 2—Issue 3 November 2009, pp. 289–302.

Rancière, Jacques. 2004 (2000).*The Politics of Aesthetics: The Distribution of the Sensible*. London, New York, Continuum International Publishing group.

Rancière, Jacques. 2007. *The Future of the Image*. London and New York: Verso.

Ray, Man. 1974 (1963). *Självporträtt.* Lund: Bo Cavefors Bokförlag.

Sartre, Jean-Paul. 2005. (1940) *The Imaginary: A phenomenological psychology of the imagination*. New York, London: Routledge.

Sassoon, Joanna. 2007. Photographic Meaning in the Age of Digital Reproduction. I: *Archives & Social Studies: A Journal of Interdisciplinary Research Vol. 1, no. 0 (March 2007).*

Sekula, Allan. 1982. On the Invention of Photographic Meaning. I: Burgin (ed.) *Thinking Photography.* London: MacMillan. pp. 84-109.

Scott, Clive. 1999. *The Spoken Image: Photography and Language.* Eastbourne: Reaktion Books. Scott, Clive. 2007. *Street photography: from Atget to Cartier Bresson.* I.B. Tauris & Co. Ltd.

Sonesson, Göran. 1989. *Semiotics of Photography: On tracing the index.* Report 4 from the Project "Pictorial meanings in the society of information". Lund University.

Sonesson, Göran. 1999. Post-photography and beyond: From mechanical reproduction to digital production. I: *Visio, 4,1 Spring 1999: Postphotography. Sonesson, Göran, (ed.), 11-36.*

Sontag, Susan. 1973. *On photography.* New York: Farrar, Straus and Giroux.

Sztompka, Piotr. 2008. The Focus on Everyday Life: a New Turn in Sociology. I: *European Review,* Vol. 16, No. 1, 1–15, 2008, Academia Europæa.

Sturken, Marita & Cartwright, Lisa. 2001. *Practices of looking: an introduction to visual culture*. Oxford: Oxford University Press.

Toffler,Alvin. 1980. *The Future Shock: The Third Wave.* New York: Bantam Books.

Tomanić Trivundža, Ilija. 2014. Records of Facts or Records of Mystification? Brief Notes on the "Surplus Value" of the Photographic Image. I: *Media Practice and Everyday Agency in Europe*. edited by Leif Kramp, Nico Carpentier, Andreas Hepp, Ilija Tomanic Trivundža, Hannu Nieminen, Risto Kunelius, Tobias Olsson, Ebba Sundin and Richard Kilborn. Bremen: edition lumière.

Trachtenberg, Alan (ed.), 1980. *Classic Essays on Photography,* New Haven: Leete's Island Books.

Örnebring, Henrik. 2008. The Consumer as Producer – of what? User-generated tabloid content in The Sun (UK) and Aftonbladet (Sweden). I: *Journalism Studies*, Vol. 9, No 5, 2008, 771-785.

Other sources

Meddelanden från K. Kommerskollegii avdelning för arbetsstatistik. 1903. Stockholm P. A. Norstedt & Söner.

Gilden, Bruce. 2015. http://www.brucegilden.com/ (Accessed 2015-04-30)

Sontag, Susan. 2014. http://www.dn.se/kultur-noje/susan-sontag-ger-har-i-fjorton-punkter-sin-estetik-i-mikroformat/ (Accessed 2015-04-03)